CONCILIUM

CONCILIUM
ADVISORY COMMITTEE

REGINA AMMICHT-QUINN	GERMANY
MARÍA PILAR AQUINO	USA
MILE BABIĆ OFM	BOSNIA–HERZEGOVINA
JOSÉ OSCAR BEOZZO	BRAZIL
WIM BEUKEN	BELGIUM
MARIA CLARA BINGEMER	BRAZIL
LEONARDO BOFF	BRAZIL
ERIK BORGMAN OP	HOLLAND
CHRISTOPHE BOUREUX OP	FRANCE
LISA SOWLE CAHILL	USA
JOHN COLEMAN	USA
EAMONN CONWAY	IRELAND
MARY SHAW COPELAND	USA
ENRICO GALAVOTTI	ITALY
DENNIS GIRA	FRANCE
NORBERT GREINACHER	GERMANY
GUSTAVO GUTIÉRREZ OP	PERU
HILLE HAKER	USA
HERMANN HÄRING	GERMANY
LINDA HOGAN	IRELAND
DIEGO IRRARÁZAVAL CSC	CHILE
WERGNER G. JEANROND	SWEDEN
JEAN-PIERRE JOSSUA OP	FRANCE
MAUREEN JUNKER-KENNY	IRELAND
FRANÇIOS KABASELE LUMBALA	DEMOCRATIC REPUBLIC OF CONGO
HANS KARL-JOSEPH KUSCHEL	GERMANY
SOLANGE LEFEBVRE	CANADA
MARY-JOHN MANANZAN	PHILIPPINES
DANIEL MARGEURAT	SWITZERLAND
ALBERTO MELLONI	ITALY
NORBERT METTE	GERMANY
DIETMAR MIETH	GERMANY
JÜRGEN MOLTMANN	GERMANY
PAUL D. MURRAY	UK
SAROJINI NADAR	(SOUTH AFRICA)
TERESA OKURE	NIGERIA
AGBONKHIANMEGHE OROBATOR SJ	KENYA
ALOYSIUS PIERIS SJ	SRI LANKA
SUSAN A. ROSS	USA
GIUSEPPE RUGGIERI	ITALY
LÉONARD SANTEDI KINKUPI	DEMOCRATIC REPUBLIC OF CONGO
SILVIA SCATENA	ITALY
PAUL SCHOTSMANS	BELGIUM
ELISABETH SCHÜSSLER FIORENZA	USA
JOHN SOBRINO SJ	EL SALVADOR
JANET MARTIN SOSKICE	UK
LUIZ CARLOS SUSIN OFM	BRAZIL
ELSA TAMEZ	COSTA RICA
CHRISTOPH THEOBALD SJ	FRANCE
ANDRÉS TORRES QUIERUGA	SPAIN
DAVID TRACEY	USA
ROBERTO TUCCI	ITALY
MARCIANO VIDAL	SPAIN
JŌAO J. VILA-CHÃ SJ	PORTUGAL
MARIE-THERES WACKER	GERMANY
ELAIN M. WAINWRIGHT	NEW ZEALAND
FELIX WILFRED	INDIA
ELLEN VAN WOLDE	HOLLAND
CHRISTOS YANNARÁS	GREECE
JOHANNES ZIZIOULAS	TURKEY

CONCILIUM 2022/1

New Developments in Theology in Asia

Edited by

Huang Po Ho, Daniel F. Pilario, Catherine Cornille, Stephan Van Erp, Tran Van Doan

Published in 2022 by SCM Press, 3rd Floor, Invicta House, 108–114 Golden Lane, London EC1Y 0TG.

SCM Press is an imprint of Hymns Ancient & Modern Ltd (a registered charity) 13A Hellesdon Park Road, Norwich NR6 5DR, UK

Copyright © International Association of Conciliar Theology, Madras (India)

www.concilium.in

English translations copyright © 2022 Hymns Ancient & Modern Ltd.

All rights reserved. No part of this publication may be reproduced, stored in a retrieval system, or transmitted, in any form or by any means, electronic, mechanical, photocopying or otherwise, without the prior written permission of the Board of Directors of Concilium.

ISBN 978-0-334-06322-3

Concilium is published in March, June, August, October, December

Contents

Editorial   7

Part One: General Approaches to Asian Theology

Asian Christian Theologies: Present Tasks and
Future Orientations   11
PETER C. PHAN

Theologies in Asia and Asian Theologies. A Radical Paradigm
Shift of Doing Theologies from Contexts   22
HUANG PO HO

Asian Theology and the Particularity of Christianity   33
CATHERINE CORNILLE

Part 2. Inculturation of Christianity in Particular Asian Contexts

Paying Attention to Indian Tantric Buddhism   47
THIERRY-MARIE COURAU

A Metaphysical Approach to Theology in Taiwan: Dialogues
between Catholicism and Daoist Teachings of Laozi and Zhuangzi   58
KATIA LENEHAN

Productive Imagination in the Story Theology of
Choan-Seng Song   67
YA-TANG CHUANG

Asian Liberation Theologies in Times of Populism 76
DANIEL F. PILARIO

Vietnamese Theology in the Making 87
TRAN VAN DOAN

Biblical Interpretation in India from Subaltern Perspectives 96
ANTONY JOHN BAPTIST

Part 3. Asian Questions and Approaches to Christian Ethics

Catholic Theological Ethics in Asia: From Conflict to
Conversation 107
MARIA JOHN P. SELVAMANI

Women Decolonizing Theologies of, for and by
Southeast Asians 117
SHARON A. BONG

Part 4. Theological forum

Catholicity as a Principle for a Dissenting Church 129
WILIBALDUS GAUT

Johann Baptist Metz (1926-2019). A Personal and Critical
Tribute 135
ERIK BORGMAN

Editorial

Theologies in Asia, Asian Theologies

Theology in Asia is constantly on the move, engaging local cultural developments, resisting Western and colonial domination, and exploring new ways of imagining and expressing the teachings of the Gospel. Though, or because Christianity is a minority religion in most Asian countries, it has been forced, more than in most other continents, to reflect self-critically on what it has to offer and how it is to relate to other religions and to secular culture. In those respects, it has much to offer to the rest of the theological world.

While we often think of contextual theology as relevant only for a particular culture or historical context, many social, ethical and theological questions and problems similarly affect Christians throughout the world. The articles in this volume on end of life questions and on gender dynamics are current in theological ethics everywhere. And the question of how to confront the reality of populism also affects Christians worldwide. The answers to these questions by Asian theologians may at times be distinctive, exposed as they are to different cultural realities and religious influences. But that is precisely what makes Asian theology, and all contextual theology interesting and important for the rest of the Christian world to engage.

Peter Phan lays out what is distinctive about Asian theology, reminding us from the outset that Asia is more internally diverse than most continents. Some of the common challenges for Asian theology are poverty, migration, colonization, religious pluralism, minority status, atheism, and ecological degeneration, each calling for their own type of theological response. Huang Po-Ho calls attention to the fact that Asian culture is not different from or "other" or "alien" with regard to the Gospel, as if Western culture would be the natural or normal habitat for Christianity. Asian theology must thus understand the process of contextualization as one of discovering its own already innate Christian identity, and thus re-confessing Christian faith. With its centuries of experience as a minority religion, Christianity in Asia has abundant experience in reflecting on

Editorial

the particularity of Christianity and what it may have to offer to local cultures and traditions. Catherine Cornille discusses various ways in which engagement with Asian religious traditions may shed new light on the distinctiveness of Christianity and thus help to shift the discussion from traditional *a priori* ideas of the uniqueness of Christianity to an *a posteriori* realization of the particularity of Christianity.

Part two of this volume focuses on concrete examples of the inculturation of Christianity in various Asian contexts. All of the contributions focus on current realities and examples, from the engagement with Daoist thought among Christian theologians in Taiwan to a subaltern Indian approach to Biblical interpretation, and from a discussion of the story theology of Choan Seng Song to an appeal to do theology in Vietnam from the lived experience of the Vietnamese people, or the need to develop a new form of liberation theology in the Philippines that confronts the challenges of populism. As the presence of Tantric Buddhism is one of the common features of Asian cultures, Thierry-Marie Courau emphasizes the urgent need for Christianity to engage this particular type of Buddhism in a constructive theological way.

Though certain ethical questions are similarly alive and pressing in different parts of the world, Asian Christianity faces these questions in a particular way as a minority religion within cultures shaped by particular social values and mores. The contributions to this volume by Selvamani and Bong are therefore all the more striking in that they express bold and prophetic positions on social and ethical issues of gender, sexual orientation, and end-of-life issues.

Together, the articles in this volume illustrate that the more grounded theology is in a local culture, the more relevant it may be for global theology. To be sure, the primary audience of Asian theology are the people of Asia, and the primary goal of Asian theology is to make Christian theology intelligible and inspiring within an Asian context. But as these articles bear out, Christianity has much to learn not only from the way in which Asian theologians engage the Asian cultures, but also from the fruits of that engagement.

Catherine Cornille, Huang Po Ho, Stephan Van Erp, Daniel Pilario,
Tran Van Doan

Part One: General Approaches to Asian Theology

Asian Christian Theologies: Present Tasks and Future Orientations

PETER C. PHAN

The article first highlights seven common elements of Asian Christianities, namely, foreignness, colonialist legacy, extreme poverty, ecological degradation, minority status, co-existence with communist and socialist regimes, and ubiquitous migration. The second part suggests a method for developing Asian Christian theologies, with a triple mediation: social-analytic, hermeneutical, and practical mediations. Extreme poverty calls for a liberationist theology; ubiquitous migration a theology of God as the Primordial Migrant; colonialist legacy an inculturated theology; minority status a theology in dialogue with other religions; the presence of communist and atheist regimes a new theology of mission; Pentecostal/Charismatic presence a vigorous pneumatology; and ecological degradation a theology of care for the Earth.

As a contribution to the construction of a theology that is not only done in Asia but is also *of* Asia, this essay begins with a brief survey of the common features of contemporary Christianity in Asia. 'Asia' here refers only to South Asia, East Asia, and Southeast Asia. The second part discusses the present tasks of an Asian theology and proposes some articulations of the Christian faith that are appropriate to the Asian contexts and can assist the Church in carrying out its mission in Asia.

Contextual Elements of Asian Christianties

Culturally, there are two dominant cultures in Asia, the Indic and the Sinic, the former predominantly in South Asia, and the latter predominantly in

East and Southeast Asia, but both cultures are present in all three regions of Asia. Politically, while there are democratic countries such as India, South Korea, Japan, Thailand, the Philippines, Malaysia, and Indonesia, their democracy has been very fragile, especially in the last four countries, as extremist groups emerged as an alternative to electoral politics. Religious freedom is also threatened by authoritarian, one-party, and/or military governments such as China, North Korea, Vietnam, Myanmar, Laos, and Brunei.

To elaborate a Christian theology appropriate to Asia as a whole it is helpful to highlight some key common elements of Christianities in the three regionseven though it is necessary to pay close attention to the socio-political, economic, cultural, and religious contexts in which Christianity exists, not only in each of the three regions but also in each country.[1]

First, it has often been said that Christianity in Asia was and remains a foreign religion that was imported by Western missionaries. Historically, this is true of Christianity in all three regions of Asia. Christianity was brought to Asia by missionaries from Portugal (India, China, Macau, Vietnam, and Timor-Leste), Spain (the Philippines), the Netherlands (Taiwan and Indonesia), Britain (India, Hong Kong, Malaysia, and Singapore), France (Vietnam, Cambodia, Laos, and Thailand), and the United States (South Korea, Myanmar, and the Philippines). Perhaps the point of the observation about the foreign character of Christianity is that Christianity has not been thoroughly indigenized into the local cultures and contexts like other Asian religions and that some Christian denominations are currently still dependent on foreign financial aid and administrative authorities and do not subscribe to the Three-Self Principles, namely, self-governing, self-supporting, and self-propagating.[2] This is especially true of the Catholic Church, with its organizational and juridical ties to the Vatican City State.

Secondly, connected with the foreignness of Christianity is the historical alliance between Christianity and colonialism in Asia. Missionaries from Portugal, Spain, Britain, France, and the United States came to evangelize Asian countries with the financial and political support of their colonizing countries. A notable example of the collusion between secular power and Church authorities is the system of royal patronage instituted in the fifteenth century between the Catholic Church on the one hand and Spain (*patronato real*) and Portugal (*padroado real*) on the other whereby in exchange for the free use of transportation to mission countries, financial subsidy for the building of churches and the maintenance of missionaries, and military protection for Christian missions, the two royal Crowns would have the privilege to appoint candidates for the episcopacy and other high ecclesiastical offices in their newly discovered and conquered territories in Latin America and Asia. No doubt the Catholic Church benefited much from this arrangement; indeed, without the assistance of the Iberian empires, it would be very unlikely that the Church could have carried out its evangelizing mission in the new worlds of Latin America and Asia. Asian Christians must honestly acknowledge the colonial legacy of their Churches and the many privileges accrued to them, especially in terms of education, health care, and social services, as the best schools, universities, hospitals, and social institutions in their countries are owned or administered by Christians.

The third common feature of Asian Christianity is its existence amidst overwhelming poverty. While South Korea, Taiwan, Hong Kong, and Singapore are the four economic 'Asian Tigers' thanks to their rapid economic growth and an improved standard of living, and although Indonesia, Malaysia, Thailand, and Vietnam have recently reached the status of economic 'Tiger Cubs', there are still millions of Asians living below poverty level, subsisting on less than US$ 1.90 a day, and having little access to education, health care, and social services. Massive poverty is also worsened by the endemic corruption and graft by kleptocratic governments that steal public funds earmarked for the betterment of the living standards in their countries. Furthermore, while globalization has raised the living standards in several Asian countries, its neoliberal market economy has widened the gap between the rich and the poor. This new form of colonialism is no less destructive of human dignity and human rights than the old one. Indeed, neocolonialism is more dangerous as its impact is not as visible as the old-time colonizers' occupation of their lands and exploitation of their natural resources. One of the most pernicious effects of the neoliberal economy is consumerism, which is the siren's song to youth and enslaves the consumers as they accumulate more and more things.

The fourth common element is ecological degradation in many Asian countries. There is an urgent need for Asian Christians to grasp the causal connection between the release of greenhouse gases (carbon dioxide, methane, nitrogen oxides, and others) into the atmosphere, the depletion of the ozone layer, global warming, the melting of the polar ice, the rise of the sea level on the one hand and human activities such as the burning of fossil fuel (coal, petroleum, and gas), deforestation, the dumping of industrial and nuclear waste and chemical products, and the increasing use of fertilizers, insecticides, fungicides, herbicides and agrotoxins on the other. The common tendency to attribute ecological destruction and natural disasters to divine punishment must be resisted. In addition, many Asian countries, for example, Indonesia and the Philippines, are located in the 'ring of fire', with devastating volcanic eruptions. Furthermore, countries with a high percentage of their population living near rivers and the coastlines are frequent victims of the effects of climate change such as tsunami, floods, and droughts that destroy the poor's livelihood and force them to migrate.

The fifth common feature of Christianity is its minority status in all Asian countries, except the Philippines and Timor-Leste. Asian Christians exist in Muslim-majority (Pakistan, Bangladesh, Malaysia, Indonesia, and Brunei), Hindu-majority (India), and Buddhist majority (South Korea, Thailand, Cambodia, Laos, Vietnam, and Sri Lanka) countries. This minority status makes dialogue with the followers of other religions an existential imperative for Asian Christians.

The sixth common feature of some Asian countries is co-existence with Communism. In self-declared Communist countries such as China, Vietnam, and North Korea, Christianity is no longer targeted for eradication as such but the Churches must be registered with the government, and their activities are regulated and restricted under the pretext of "national security" and "social unity." In China, in particular, the Catholic Church must deal with the problem of two parallel Churches, the so-called official or registered Church and the underground or unregistered Church, especiallythe thorny issue of the nomination and ordination of bishops. In authoritarian countries, often under military regimes, religious repression and violations of human rights are committed not in the name of ideology but to maintain the government's absolute power. In Muslim-majority countries such as Pakistan, Brunei, Indonesia, and Malaysia, religious freedom is constitutionally guaranteed but in practice, legal restrictions on religious practices are put in place against Christians. Even in democratic countries such as India, Malaysia, and Indonesia, especially when right-wing political movements and religious extremists are in power, there are the blasphemy law and prohibitions against conversion from Islam and Hinduism, the use of the term Allah for the Christian God, the distribution of bibles, missionary activities, and public celebration of Christian feasts.

The seventh common feature of Asian countries is ubiquitous migration. In the last fifty years, Asia has massively entered the global migration age. Rapid economic growth, the impact of globalization, social transformations, international and civil wars, and ecological disasters have accelerated the rate of migration of Asians from Asian countries to non-Asian countries, to other Asian countries (international migrants), and also within each country (internally displaced persons), especially due to the movement of people from rural areas to the cities in search of work (urbanization). From the end of World War II and the dismantling of British, French, Dutch, and Japanese colonial empires to 1973, there were waves of returning colonists, often with their families of colonial subjects, to their respective countries, especially from Indonesia to Holland, from Vietnam to France, from Timor-Leste to Portugal, and from India to Britain. Also during these three decades, there were protracted wars in Korea and Vietnam that caused millions of people to leave the north for the south. During 1975-1989, after the Oil Boom, the Gulf region emerged as the new migration destination for Asian migrants, especially from India, Pakistan, and the Philippines. The end of the Vietnam War, with the victory of Communist North Vietnam over South Vietnam in 1975, saw hundreds of thousands of Vietnamese, Cambodians, and Laotians migrate to the U.S., Canada, Australia, and European countries. During 1989-2008, the increasing demand for lower- and higher-skilled workers in the Gulf region attracted a large number of Asian migrants. Also, there was intra-regional migration from poorer Southeast Asian countries like Indonesia, Vietnam, and the Philippines to richer Southeast Asian countries like Malaysia, Singapore, and Thailand and East Asian countries such as China, Japan, South Korea, and Taiwan. Since 2008 there has been an acceleration of extra-regional migration, especially from Indonesia and Myanmar, to the Gulf, North America, and Europe, and intra-regional migration, especially to East Asia and some countries of Southeast Asia. Recently there has been a forced displacement of Rohyngis from Myanmar and Uyghurs in Northwest China.

The eighth common feature of Asian countries is the oppressed status of women, economically, socio-politically, culturally, and religiously. Though significant improvements in women's condition have been made in several countries thanks to their struggle for equal rights, there are still severe restrictions based on their gender in education, employment, political rights, and religious functions, especially in Muslim-majority countries and those with patriarchal cultures. The Christian Churches in Asia as a whole have exacerbated this anti-woman ethos with their male-dominated structures and practices.

Future Asian Theologies: Tasks and Orientations
Christian theology is the critical and systematic understanding of Jesus' message about the reign of God as it is communicated and lived by the Church in different times and places. There are thus two constitutive elements in the making of theology, one that is constant and permanent and the other by nature changeable and varied, namely, Jesus' message and its transmission and practice by Christians in various contexts respectively. Of course, Jesus' message, though permanent and constant, is not a context-free reality descending straight from heaven as it were; rather, like the eternal Son of God made flesh as a Jew in Palestine, his message, as recorded in the New Testament, is already contextualized in different cultures, namely, Jewish and Greek. Consequently, it is more accurate to understand theology as an intercontextual or intercultural critical study of the encounter between the cultures in which Jesus' message has been embodied and the new cultures in which it is to be inculturated again. There are in theology both the transcendent or universal message of Jesus about the reign of God and the historicized or particular realization of that message at different times and in various locations throughout the world.

Doing theology in this way involves three interrelated steps. The first step, which may be called the "socio-analytic mediation" of the theological discipline, seeks to ascertain the empirical facts as they are, as objectively and as truthfully as possible, as the context for theology. That is what has been done in the first two sections of this article. The second step, which may be called the "hermeneutical mediation", interprets the empirical data in the light of the Bible and Christian Tradition; and vice versa, it interprets the Bible and the Christian Tradition in the light of the empirical data obtained in the socio-analytic mediation to yield a theological hypothesis or theory. The third step, the "practical mediation," seeks to embody the theological answer in the practice of the Christian community, which practice, in turn, generates new data for the socio-analytic mediation, and the processes of theological hermeneutic mediation and practical mediation begin all over again. In what follows, it is not of course possible to elaborate the hermeneutical and practical mediations of an Asian theology in detail. I will only indicate some of the tasks and orientations of such a theology in the light of the data discussed above.

First, the widespread and dehumanizing poverty in several Asian countries must be the constant concern of Asian Churches and postcolonialist theology. This poverty has been exacerbated by neocolonialist globalization, government corruption, anti-democratic militaristic regime, increasing urbanization, and ecological degradation, which prevent social, political, and economic projects from attaining their goals of bringing about well-being to the most marginalized citizens. The work of abolishing poverty and promoting justice, which is an intrinsic part of the mission of the Church, is known as liberation or integral human development. In defense of and solidarity with the poor and the marginalized, the Federation of Asian Bishops' Conferences (FABC) repeatedly advocates the "dialogue with the poor" which consists of the Church's "option for the poor" and solidarity with them to achieve their liberation from structural injustice and oppression. In this struggle for social justice, the poor themselves act as agents of their liberation and are not just victims and beneficiaries of the charity of others. This struggle for justice is also emphasized by the Christian Conference of Asia (CCA), a regional ecumenical organization representing National Councils and over 100 denominations as well as by the Asia Evangelical Alliance (AEA), whose goal is said to be "to promote and nurture unity, collaborations and cooperation among ministry organizations, church networks and primarily the National Evangelical Alliances within Asia and with those outside Asia for the purpose of building, strengthening and expanding the Kingdom of God in Asia and beyond."[3]

Second, connected with poverty is the issue of migration. Several Asian countries are countries of emigration, especially Pakistan, Nepal, the Philippines, Vietnam, Indonesia, and Myanmar. Churches must set up programs to prepare emigrants before their departure, connect with them while they are abroad, and assist the families that are left behind. Emigration cannot be eliminated, but efforts must be made by both the government and the Churches to reduce the "culture of emigration", the feminization of labor export, sex trafficking, and the misuse of remittances in the emigration countries. Theologically, a theology of migration must be elaborated in which God is shown to be the Primordial Migrant, Jesus the Paradigmatic Migrant, the Holy Spirit the Power of Migration, and the Church as a community of migrants.

Third, the work to make Christianity a truly Asian religion through comprehensive inculturation or contextualization, already well underway in several countries, for example, India, South Korea, and the Philippines, should be assiduously continued and expanded to all aspects of the church life in all countries. Here theology has an irreplaceable role. Beyond classical resources such as philosophy and religion, such theological inculturation must take into account the socio-political and economic contexts, cultural artifacts, and digital social media. In this way, Asian Christianity can effectively shed its colonial heritage and its foreign character. While Protestants, Evangelicals, and Pentecostals devote their resources to translating the Bible into hundreds of local languages, Catholics focus on adapting the liturgy and worship to the local cultures, making use of indigenous music, song, dance, rituals, practices of popular religion, and customs. A theology of inculturation must be developed in which the relation between the Gospel and culture is carefully analyzed, the dynamic equivalences between the Christian beliefs and the beliefs of other religions explored, and the ways to express and live the Christian faith in different local contexts put into practice.

Fourth, interreligious dialogue must be seriously undertaken in Christian-majority as well as Christian-minority countries. This is done in four areas, as frequently advocated by the FABC, namely, sharing daily life, collaboration for the common good, theological reflection, and sharing spiritual experiences. This interreligious dialogue not only promotes a deeper understanding and acceptance of the religious "Other" but is also an effective means to reduce religious extremism, radicalism, and violence in Asia. A theology of interreligious dialogue must go beyond the three paradigms of exclusivism, inclusivism, and pluralism in which Christianity is taken as the norm to evaluate the truth and value of other religions which are judged to be true and holy only to the extent they conform to Christianity, to be "fulfilled" by it, or as merely stepping-stones to Christianity. Rather, the dialogue among the religions must be a sincere, respectful, and humble undertaking to witness truthfully to others what one believes and practices without claiming that one's religion is the only true one or the best, a claim that is epistemologically impossible to prove. It must involve a readiness to share with others the truths and values of one's religion, to learn from the truths and practices of the religions of the partners-in-dialogue, to correct the errors and deficiencies of one's religion, and to be complemented and enriched by others.

Fifth, related to the issues of liberation, inculturation, and interreligious dialogue is the nature of the Christian mission. Mission or evangelism is understood and practiced very differently by Christians in Asia. Evangelicals, Pentecostals/Charismatics, and Independents understand mission as consisting mainly in preaching to non-Christians with the ultimate goal of converting and baptizing them. As mentioned above, this kind of mission is prohibited in some Muslim-majority countries. On the other hand, other Churches understand mission as bearing witness, by word and deed, to the Christian faith with the goal not primarily to convert non-Christian individuals, though this is not excluded, but to bring the reality and values of God's kingdom to the world. Christian mission is not only *missio ad gentes*, with non-Christians as the objects of the Christian's evangelism but also, and above all, *missio inter gentes*, that is, a mutual mission to one another, with Christians and non-Christians "converting" one another toward the kingdom of God, and *missio cum gentibus*, that is, mission carried by Christians together with non-Christians for the coming of the reign of God. This dialogue is particularly urgent between Christians and Muslims in Asia as both religions are forecast to be the two major religions in Asia. A peaceful relation between the two groups is essential for the well-being of Asia, especially in countries such as India, Thailand, the Philippines, and Indonesia.

Sixth, given the enormous growth of Evangelicals, Pentecostals/

Charismatics, and Independents in Asia, a robust theology of the Holy Spirit (pneumatology) is urgently needed, not only for the dialogue between them and the other branches of Christianity (ecumenical dialogue) but also for a positive appreciation of the role of non-Christian religions in God's plan of salvation (interreligious dialogue). In Catholic theology, in Asia as well as elsewhere, a Christocentric, even Christonomic theology has been developed extensively; as a result, an exclusivist approach is usually adopted in the theology of religion. To redress the balance, a pneumatological Christology or Christological pneumatology is urgently needed to acknowledge the salvific presence of God in non-Christian religions. In this way, St. Irenaeus's celebrated image of God the Father (*Theos*) acting in the world always with two hands, the Word (*Logos*) and the Spirit (*Pneuma*), and not one *or* the other, is made into the leitmotif of Christian theology.

Seventh, the widespread destruction of the environment in almost all Asian countries by both natural catastrophes and human abuses of natural resources which produces climate change and global warming urgently calls for a comprehensive theology of creation and ecology that moves beyond "natural" and human/social" ecology to "integral" ecology. In this respect, Pope Francis's encyclical *Laudato Si'* is a magna carta that provides rich insights on solidarity, sustainability, and subsidiarity; on the links among ecology, migration, economics, and politics; on capitalism, consumerism, and the "throwaway culture"; on work and human relationships; on technology, energy, and recycling; and on food and water.

Eighth, though a vibrant feminist theology has been developed in Asia, especially in India, the Philippines, and Korea, it is far from gaining widespread acceptance and has not been made an integral part of the theological curriculum in almost all Christian denominations, notably the Catholic, Orthodox, Evangelical, and Pentecostal Churches. The necessity of feminist theology for Asia is made all the more urgent by the fact Church life is nurtured by a large number of female workers, though mostly in subordinate positions. Such feminist theology should not derive its inspiration only from Western theories but also from abundant Asian resources, both cultural and religious.

In conclusion, a Christian theology that is appropriate for South, East, and Southeast Asia must begin from their contemporary socio-political, economic, cultural, and religious contexts and the common challenges that these contexts pose to Christianity. Christian theology interprets these data in the light of the Gospel and the Gospel in the light of these data. I contend that to meet the challenges of Asia today contemporary Asian theology must develop a theology of liberation, migration, inculturation, interreligious dialogue, mission, the Holy Spirit, ecology, and feminist theology. I am fully aware that these theologies have been widely developed by Asian theologians and my enumeration of these theologies here is not so much for their benefit as for Western theologians that are less familiar with them. I have indicated the main outlines and orientations of these eight theologies, with the full awareness that they should be adapted to the particular conditions of each region and each country.[4]

Notes

1. On Christianity in Asia, see Kenneth R. Ross, Daniel Jayaraj, and Todd M. Johnson (eds.), *South and Central Asia*. Edinburgh: Edinburgh University Press, 2019 and Kenneth R. Ross, Francis D. Alvarez, and Todd M. Johnson (eds.), *Christianity in East and Southeast Asia*. Edinburgh: Edinburgh University Press, 2020.
2. The "Three-Self Principles" were first proposed in missiological circles in the late nineteenth centuryby Henry Venn and Rufus Anderson and are also known as the "Nevius Method" as it was also proposed by John Livingstone Nevius, a missionary to China and Korea. They were much discussed in China and were adopted by the Protestant Churches as the foundation of the "Three-Self Patriotic Movement."
3. See https://asiaevangelicals.org [19 June 2021].
4. Note that I have not mentioned a specific theology in response to Communist and right-wing ideologies, and this is of set purpose. I do not believe that the most effective counter-response to these ideologies is a theoretical discussion of the metaphysical "proofs" of God's existence and human rights. Rather the Church's convincing "argument" for the belief in God and against right-wing ideology is a relentless struggle for equality and justice, especially in favor of the poor and the oppressed.

Theologies in Asia and Asian Theologies - A Radical Paradigm Shift of Doing Theology from Contexts

HUANG PO HO

This paper is trying to discern the conceptual differences between Theologies in Asia and Asian theologies, with an attempt to highlight the distinctive characteristics of "Asian Theologies", stressing on its shift of resources and methodologies. The paper has reflected on the colonial nature of most theologies in Asia, and the way that Asian theologies were developed and their struggle to be genuinely Asian.

1. Introduction
Theology if understood as "persistent struggling to discern the Human-Divine relations for Life Transformation"[1], is a daily experience and desire of human society. Theologies in Asia thus can be dated back to the genesis of human creation. Asia as the homeland of all existing world religions[2] is a continent full of religiosity, and its people are used to appraise their life struggles with different deities. It is a land with deep spiritualities and flourishing theologies.

However, the common tragic historical fate of colonization, dictatorial oppression and exploitation of the Asian continent have sculpted Asian religions to become survival religions. In effect, these differing spiritualities also tend to provide utilitarian and pragmatic practices that sustain people's lives in the midst of external threat and danger. There were of course, prophetic advocacies voiced out from these religions in different circumstances. They were however vulnerable to suppression by dominant political forces.

2. Christianity as a Hybrid Religion

Christianity is one of the Asian religions that emerged out of Judaism in Palestine of West Asia. Though there were numerous footprints that spread in Asia during the early Christian history, its mainstream mission was directed toward Western world by the great missionary preacher St. Paul. Ever since, Christianity has been considered a Western religion; it was only brought back to Asia accompanied by two waves of Western colonial movements during 16th and 18th century.

This particular journey has created tremendous impacts to the Christian religion, and made the Christian faith a hybrid religious system constituted by both Eastern and Western cultural elements. Watsuji Tetsurō (1889–1960), one of philosophers in Japan during the twentieth century who brought Japanese philosophy to the world,[3] made an interesting observation on the interrelations between climate, culture and religion. In his famous work of "A Climate" (*Fudo*),[4] Watsuji Tetsuro recognizes that the world is an always already meaningful place for us. Part of his inspiration is Heidegger, and his conviction is that Heidegger's focus on time considered only part of the story. Watsuji sees place and space as just as determinative of human consciousness and culture as time.[5] For him, *fudo* becomes a way of differentiating several different national characters. His three basic climate types, monsoon, desert, and meadow, correspond to different world cultures. The monsoon type includes Japan, China, India, and the rest of the coastal belt of Asia. The desert type refers to Arabia, Africa, and Mongolia. The meadow type mainly refers to Europe.[6] Recognizing that the birth place of Christianity was in Arabia which is a desert type of climate, he argues that the westward journey of Christianity which led it from the desert to the meadow created the first paradigm shift of the Christian faith through its hybrid struggle in between:

> When Paul's Christianity, with its Jewish content, was growing up in the European world, although there was a rejection of the dryness of Judaism, the product of the desert, the moral passion of the prophets came to be more and more an integral part. And at the same time, in that the dampness that is not found in the desert became the feature of Christianity in Europe, the gentleness of the religion of love grew very strong. It would not be untrue to say that the worship of the Virgin Mary

is much more of monsoon than of desert pattern.[7]

When tracing the journey of this desert-born Christianity which being nurtured thousand years under the meadow culture of Europe, and later being brought back to east Asia a monsoon climate region, Watsuji again alerts its cultural and spiritual challenges:

> Thus, to these (monsoon) people, the world becomes a place teeming with plant and animal life; for them, nature is not death but life, for death stands, instead, by the side of man. Hence, the relation between man and his world is not that of resistance, but that of resignation. The drought of the desert produces a relation which is the exact opposite.[8]

Watsuji's *Climate and Culture* is both an appreciation and a critique of Heidegger. In particular, he argues that Heidegger under-emphasizes spatiality and over-emphasizes temporality. Watsuji contends that had Heidegger equally emphasized spatiality, it would have tied him more firmly to the human world where we interact, both fruitfully and negatively. We are inextricably social, connected in so many ways; and ethics is the study of these social connections and positive ways of interacting.[9] It was based on this distinctive eastern perception of spatiality against western temporality, that he was compelled to develop this concept of *fudo* to interpret the three particular climate (milieu) regions of the world.[10]

Whether one agrees or not to Watsuji's climate (*fudo*) determinism, his insightful suggestion about the historical journey of Asian Christianity that has gone through all the three types of cultural zones is undoubtedly enlightening. It points to the profundity and complexity of the Christian faith and theology as we find it in Asia. Though implicitly, he has unveiled the hybrid nature of Christian religion and its struggles to readjust and develop its doctrines, vis-à-vis its dual origins, East and West.

3. Colonial Religion and Missionary Theologies
The homecoming of the Christian religion to Asia, after spending more than a thousand years in the Western world, did not only produce a hybrid identity in its cultures and philosophies. It was also accompanied by the colonial military forces that defended political oppression and economic

exploitation of the western colonial empires.

Though there are Asian church historians who make tremendous efforts to reconstruct the early Christian missions in Asia, and gave evidences to those eastward missionary journey of the apostles and early missionaries, the existing Asian Christian churches are mostly established by Western missionaries through the two waves of European overseas colonial movements, namely 16th century and 19th centuries, when their naval forces were formidable for overseas colonization. Rarely do we see any existing Asian church today that have direct connections to those early missionary legends.

Christianity in Asia is thus perceived by Asian eyes as a colonial religion. Following the arrival of colonial political and military forces, Christian denominations and individual missionaries, already hybrid in Western world, took control of the Asian landscape. They spread Christian knowledge, built churches and established theological schools—mostly mission schools—to train local preachers as aids to Western missionaries in the work of proselytizing local peoples to their individual denominations. It is still true even today, two hundred years later after the earliest existing theological school was established in Asia. Most of the theological education are denominational training programs with missionary theologies as their main content. These theologies were created elsewhere and imported to Asia, polluting and creating divisions and conflicts to the Asian communities.

These attempts to implement foreign theological education and theological knowledge to Asian people can be dated back to a century earlier when the arrival and establishment of Christian churches by the Oriental Orthodox tradition, and later enhanced by successive Roman Catholic and Protestant Christian missions from Europe and North America.[11] Even today, the main direction of theological education carried out through institutions of professional higher education in Asia, appreciated or unappreciated, are modeled after theological schools from the Western world in their curricula, program divisions, and even in administrative structures.[12]

4. Doing Contextual Theologies in Asia
Definitions of "contextual theology" have been vague and diverse.

Generally speaking it can be classified into four types or stages, namely, transplantation, interpretation, participation and reconstruction.[13] These classifications are based on the critical role of local cultures to be treated in the theological constructions.

Influenced by Karl Barth and Hendrik Kraemer, both the zealous missionaries and local pastors who were mostly trained by the missionaries or missionaries' home theological schools in the early period of Asian Church history, believed that Gospel and cultures are two independent entities. While Gospel was considered as God's divine grace, cultures were seen as products of sinful human beings. Thus, a prevailing hostile Christian attitude toward local religions and cultures was developed. Kraemer's classic work on "The Christian Message in a Non-Christian World" which was written purposely for the meeting of the International Missionary Council at Tambaram (Madras 1938) has distinguished sharply between what he called "biblical realism" and non-Christian religious experience. His view which reflected the work of Karl Barth and Emil Brunner, evoked strong opposition in liberal circles and among Indian theologians.[14] Yet it has laid the basic foundation as the overseas missionary guidelines for the following centuries after the Tambaram council. Theology thus was considered something that can only be produced outside of Asia and imported into its land. Proselytism in this sense means to deny or even to destroy the cultures of those proselytized.

However, the post-World War II atmosphere of national independent movements and the solidarity shown from the local congregations made Asian church leaders and theologians reclaim their Asian identity and treasure more their own cultural heritages. Local cultures were taken as useful instrument to translate and interpret Christian faith. Asian theologies were formally initiated through its first phase in the program of "indigenization". Generally speaking, indigenization has employed the people's cultures as a tool to translate or interpret Christian faith and theologies that were introduced by the western churches. For instance, Kosuke Koyama, a Japanese theologian, explained that his initial theological endeavor was to subordinate the great theological thoughts of Thomas Aquinas and Karl Barth to the intellectual and spiritual need of the farmers.[15] He was enlightened by Paul's teaching about his freedom to adjust himself to the given contexts.[16] "To win people" is the key word of this passage, and it is the core value and hidden intention of the indigenization model of theology.

Shoki Coe, a Taiwanese theologian, however was dissatisfied with this utilitarian usage of local cultures and contexts. He identifies the limitation of the indigenization model as taking contexts and cultures to have static and past orientations. The editors of *Mission Trend* comments on Coe's proposal to shift indigenization to "contextualizing theology":

> In the developing theologies of the "younger churches" in the third world, the emphasis has shifted from indigenization to contextualization. Why? How do they differ? Indigenization, according to Shoki Coe, derives from the idea of "taking root in the soil", and tends to suggest a static response to the Gospel in term of traditional culture. Therefore, it is in danger of being past-oriented. The context today, however, "is not that of static culture, but the search for the new, which at the same time has involved the culture itself." Therefore, he says, "in using the word contextualization, we try to convey all that is implied in the familiar term indigenization, yet seek to press beyond for a more dynamic concept which is open to change and which is also future-oriented."[17]

Shoki Coe's contextualizing theology model was developed with his particular strategic concern of the "Missio Dei". He argues: "It is the missiological discernment of the signs of the times, seeing where God is at work and calling us to participate in it. Thus, contextuality is more than just taking all contexts seriously but indiscriminately. It is the conscientization of the contexts in the particular, historical moment, assessing the particular of the context in the light of the mission of the church as it is called to participate in the Missio Dei. Such conscientization can only come through involvement and participation out of which critical awareness may arise."[18] For Shoki, contexts and cultures are no longer simply tools or instruments to translate or interpret the defined "Gospel" but are themselves elements to be engaged "in the struggle of redefining the "Gospel" in order to properly fulfill the "Missio Dei".

5. Radical Paradigm Shift of Doing Theologies from Context
The roles of cultures and contexts have been taken by Asian theologians

as the critical criteria to assess its vitality of a living theology. Shoki Coe while stressing on the essential role of cultures and contexts for contextual theology, was aware of the critiques and challenges raised against this theological proposal. Quoting from him again, he wrote: "Dr. Jürgen Moltmann warns of the danger that academic theology may become so contextualized that it become fossilized theology, and all the more dangerous because we are not aware of it. But equally there is a danger of contextual theology becoming chameleon theology, changing color according to the contexts."[19] In responding to this challenge, Shoki Coe argued:

> Authentic contextuality leads to contextualization. The two cannot be separated, though they should be distinct. This dialectic between contextuality and contextualization indicates a new way of theologizing. It involves not only words, but actions. Through this, the inherent danger of a dichotomy between theory and practice, action and reflection, the classroom and the street should be overcome. Authentic theological reflection can only take place as the *theologia in loco,* discerning the contextuality within the concrete context. But it must also be aware that such authentic theological reflection is at best, but also at most, *theologia viatorum.*[20]

And he thus concludes that he does not speak about "contextual theology" nor "contextualized theology" but about "contextualizing theology".[21]

Derived from this contextual argument that texts and contexts are to engage and struggle to each other, the issue on relationship between Gospel and cultures was called into question. It was in the midst of this background that the Programme for Theology and Cultures in Asia (PTCA), an Asian theological movement was given birth to drive Asian theology to a radical shift in its paradigm.

The main theological thrust of PTCA is to switch the traditional theological elements to that of local resources. Its series of workshop held for the purpose of theological re-orientation to the Asian young theological teachers and Doctoral students were focused on "Doing Theology with Asian Resources"[22] whose tremendous significance was to turn away from the substances and methodologies of traditional theologies. By asserting that Asian theology should be done with Asian resources, this theological movement denies the dichotomy of the concept of Gospel and culture. Instead, it asserts that the Gospel is found in diverse cultures, and surely Asian cultures are parts and the most splendid parts of these diverse cultures.

Starting from this theological discernment of the Gospel and the recapturing of the role and meaning of local cultures and religions, PTCA along its history developed at least three radical theological attempts to characterize distinctive of Asian Theologies:[23]

1) *Cross-textual Reading of Christian scriptures*
This was introduced by Archie Lee, a Hebrew Bible scholar from Hong Kong. Taking the plural religious contexts in Asia and also recognizing that Asian cultures are also part of God's creation, Lee has proposed that Christian scriptures cannot be read in isolation from the cultural texts as well religious texts of Asia. He thus named the Asian resources as text A, and Biblical passages as text B, and suggesting a cross reading through mutual critique and illumination to attain a relevant understanding of the truth. This cross textual reading method is also intended to decolonize the western Christian interpretation of the Bible, as well to reconcile the hyphenated identity of Asian-Christian struggles.[24]

2) *Story Telling Theology*
This was articulated by C. S. Song, a Taiwanese theologian, who was one of the founding leaders of PTCA. He is one of the most prominent theologians in Asia and also well known to the world. Story Theology substitutes traditional western argumentation theology. He contends that theology is story of the people telling the passion and hope out of their suffering in their wrestling with God in order to understand the meaning of their life. Song argues that biblical passages are nothing but stories of God's people, and Jesus is himself a master storyteller.[25]

C.S. Song insists that God has done redemptive works in creation through all cultures, even the so called "non-Christian" cultures. Asian Christians are therefore obliged to articulate an Asian theology that is born from the "womb" of Asia, one which is more intuitive and story oriented rather than the Western style of logical reasoning.[26] He points out that "stories that reflect people's experiences out of their suffering, anguish and hope, are vital sources for theology to grasp people's struggling and hope."[27] Besides proposing story as resource of theology, Song also suggested storytelling to be method for doing theology.[28]

3) *Re-confessing Theology*
This is a contribution from this writer. Re-confessing model was developed with an understanding that theology as faith reflection is by nature no other than Christian confession (or profession) of faith. The act of religious confession in its genuine sense involves both Gospel and culture aspects of the struggle. Faith confession, on the one hand, has to look upon the transcendent, seeking to grasp the truth and the Gospel. On the other hand, a genuine meaningful confession can only be done by the awareness of one's identity which is also shaped by one's cultural tradition.

The re-confessing model intends to look into the paradoxical and dynamic struggle between Gospel and cultures, in the shaping of the Christian's new identity/new life ("new being" in theological term) within the context of the so called "non-Christian" world. On the one hand, we recognize that the Gospel liberates people and cultures. On the other hand, we also reconfirm that there is no Gospel without cultures and there is no culture without the Gospel. Gospel and culture are two sides of one and the same coin; they are entangled together in the process of the confession of faith and, thus, has made theology critical and vital in the midst of one's life struggles to be human.

All these theological endeavors are based on a common concern for the issue of identity of the people that theologians represent, a hyphenated identity that Asian-Christians received after being evangelized to witness to the Christian tradition. In order to reconcile these two identities, and to transform them into one authentic and integral personhood through living out their Christian mission in the "pagan" world, Asian theologies have to take up these cultures and religions as theological resources, and develop them to a new scenario of faith and Christian praxis.

To do theology in Asia is not to take local cultures and religions as an "other" opposite the Christian tradition. Instead, these so called "pagan" cultures and religions should be considered as identity shaping features of Asian peoples, and thus must be taken as essential elements of

Christian theologies. By so doing Asian resources should not be treated as an opponent for dialogue or comparison. If there is a dialogue in the theological process, it must be an inner dialogue within, struggling for the reconciliation of their hyphenated identities of being Asian-Christians. Asian contexts, in this regard, have radically shaped a new theological paradigm of Christian theologies in Asia.

Notes

1. This definition is based on C.S. Song's article of "Theology That Tells People's Passion Stories." The phrase is an interpretation of this writer to C.S. Song's arguments.
2. A common understanding of so-called world religions in academic circle are in two opinion, one considering its spreading geographies has limited them to three religion of Christianity, Islam and Buddhism, another one focus on its history, seize and influences has identify 5 religions of Judaism, Christianity, Islam, Hinduism and Buddhism. And all of them are from Asia.
3. Watsuji Tetsurō, *Stanford Encyclopedia of Philosophy*, see: https://plato.stanford.edu/ entries/ watsuji-tetsuro/#Rel. Retrieved at March 25, 2021.
4. *Fūdo (Fūdoningen-gakutekikōsatsu)*, translated into English as *Climate and Culture*. 'Fūdo' means "wind and earth…the natural environment of a given land" (Watsuji 1988 [1961], 1). see ibid.,
5. Bruce B. Janz, Watsuji Tetsuro, *Fudo and climate change*, Journal of Global Ethics Vol. 7, No. 2, August 2011, p. 176
6. *ibid.*
7. Watsuji Tetsuro, *A Climate - A Philosophical Study*, translated by Geoffry Bownas, published by Printing Bureau, Japanese Government, 1961. p. 61
8. Watsuji Tetsuro, *ibid.*, p. 39
9. Watsuji Tetsurō, *Stanford Encyclopedia of Philosophy, ibid.*
10. Citing concrete typology of religions influenced by the climate, Watsuji points out that the monotheism religion is a product of desert, pantheism from meadow while monsoon climate shaping the reincarnation religions.
11. Huang Po Ho, *Embracing the Household of God: A Paradigm Shift from Anthropocentric Tradition to Creation Responsibility in Doing Theology* (India: PTCA, 2014), p. 99
12. *ibid.*
13. Huang Po Ho, *No Longer A Stranger*, pp. 37-40
14. Tyler Lenocker, Kraemer, Hendrik (1888-1965) Dutch Reformed lay theologian, linguist, and missiologist, BU School of Theology History of Missiology (Boston University), see: http://www.bu.edu/missiology/missionary-biography/i-k/kraemer-hendrik-1888-1965/ retrieved at April 4, 2021.
15. Kosuke Koyama, *Wateruffalo Theology* (UK: CSM Press Ltd, 1974) p. viii.
16. I Cor. 8.19-23
17. Shoki Coe, 'Contextualizing Theology, Mission Trends' No. 3, *Asian, African and Latin American Contributions to a Radical, Theological Realignment in the Church*, edited by Gerald H. Anderson, Thomas F. Stransky, C.S.P., (USA: Paulist Fathers, Inc. and Wm B. Eerdmans Publishing co., 1976) p. 19.
18. *ibid.*, pp. 21-22
19. *ibid.*, 21
20. *ibid.*, p. 22
21. *ibid.*, at the time Shoki Coe was director of WCC Theological Education Fund, which under his leadership issued a third mandate for theological education to stress on Contextualization.
22. see PTCA, *Doing Theology with Asian Resources : Ten Years in the Foundation of Living Theology in*

Asia (Auckland : Pace Publishing, 1993).
23. The following sections are taken and revised from my previous book on *Embracing the Household of God*, pp. 107-108.
24. Archie Lee, 'Biblical Interpretation in Asia Perspective', *Asian Journal of Theology* 7, 1993, pp.35-39.
25. See C.S. Song, *Tell Us Our Names: Story Theology from an Asian Perspective*, (New York: Orbis books, 1984) pp. ix-x, ref. also his unpublished paper of 'Theology That Tells People's Passion Stories' which is his keynote address at the 34th Biennial meeting of the Association of Theological Schools in the United States and Canada held at Pittsburgh, Pennsylvania, June, 17-19,1984.
26. Huang Po Ho, *Embracing the Household of God*, p. 107
27. *ibid.*
28. *ibid.*

Asian Theology and the Particularity of Christianity

CATHERINE CORNILLE

As a minority religion, Christianity in Asia has a long tradition of reflecting on its distinctiveness or particularity among other religious traditions. It may thus offer insights for a more productive or constructive understanding of the uniqueness of Christianity in dialogue with other religious traditions. While the traditional theological understanding of Christian uniqueness is based on a priori *theological assumptions, this paper explores various ways in which the particularity of Christianity may be conceived in relational and* a posteriori *terms, drawing from the thinking and experience of Indian Christian theologians.*

The question of the uniqueness of Christianity has long been part of Asian theological reflection. As a minority amidst many other religions, Christian theologians have had to tread lightly on traditional claims of the exclusiveness of salvation in Jesus Christ and the Church, and the idea of the superiority of Christianity. Some have come to largely abandon any notion of uniqueness, while others have sought to rethink it in terms less offensive and in greater attunement to the truth, goodness and beauty found in other Asian religions.

The debates around Christian uniqueness have traditionally evolved from *a priori* doctrinal beliefs in the unique and universal salvific efficacy of Jesus' death and resurrection, and in the Church as the sole continuation and mediation of that salvation. The traditional paradigms of exclusivism, inclusivism, and pluralism represent an entirely logical set of deductions from those theological presuppositions. They do not say much, however about the actual particularity or distinctiveness of Christianity among the other religions of the world. The more inductive, historical and comparative approach to religions, on the other hand, focuses more on the similarities and on the non-distinctiveness of Christianity (or any other religion). The various religions are approached in terms of types or "fractals" which may be found in different religions in their own particular forms.

Neither the *a priori* postulation of uniqueness nor the erasure of distinctiveness has much to a constructive dialogue between religions. Dialogue presupposes a certain self-knowledge and awareness of what one might contribute to the dialogue while also being open to what one may learn from others. But such self-knowledge is itself often the fruit of the dialogue, of seeing oneself through the eyes of the other, and becoming aware of the particularities of one's own beliefs and practices.

I would here like to consider a new approach to the particularity of Christianity, or new ways of detecting the distinctiveness of Christianity, not in *a priori* and universal, but in relational and contextual terms. There are at least four ways in which such distinctiveness may be discovered in dialogue: through Christian remnants in experiences of religious hybridity, through "holy envy" coming from members of other religions, and through the insights of contextual theologians who have spent a lifetime engaging other religious traditions. To be sure, the distinctiveness or particularity of Christianity may be seen to include every single aspect of the tradition, as every teaching and practice is colored by the overall particularity or singularity of Christian faith and history. Moreover, what is distinctive about Christianity may not only include its most laudable or admirable traits. We will here however focus on those elements of Christian particularity which may represent a distinctive contribution to the dialogue with other religions. Since we approach Christian particularity in relational and contextual terms, varying elements of the distinctiveness of Christianity may come to the fore in different contexts. The focus here will be predominantly on the Indian subcontinent, and on the dialogue with Hinduism and Buddhism.

1. Dual Belonging and Christian Particularity
One of the religious phenomena that has only recently come to the

attention of scholars in the West, but that has been part of Asian religiosity for centuries, is that of multiple religious belonging or religious hybridity, the personal identification with more than one religion. This has been commonplace in China and in Japan, and in more transient forms throughout Asia as individuals faced with a certain crisis tend to turn to whatever religion might resolve the problem.

With a greater openness toward other religious traditions, Christian theologians have also at times been deeply drawn to other religions, in particular Hinduism and Buddhism, often openly confessing a sense of partial identification with them. Famous Christian dual belongers are the French Benedictine monk Henri Le Saux/ Abhishitananda, who came to also deeply identify with the non-dual tradition of Hinduism, Raimon Panikkar, who claimed to have started out as Christian, became a Hindu, then a Buddhist, without having ceased to be Christian, and Aloysius Pieris, who has been called an "unremarkable hybrid" in so far as "plurality is so deeply ingrained in Asia, in Christianity, and in religion itself as to make the very notion of multiple belonging redundant."[1] In many cases, dual belongers or religious hybrids are strongly drawn to another religion, while unable to completely abandon their native religious tradition. While this may at times result from nostalgia for familiar rituals or family traditions, it may also involve genuine conviction of the truth or validity of certain teachings and practices one would not want to abandon in spite of the appeal of the other religion.

Abhishiktananda was mainly intent on deepening Christianity through the integration of the teachings and practices of *Advaita Vedanta*. While he goes far in reinterpreting Christianity and the uniqueness of Jesus in Hindu terms, he also affirms that "Christianity is the revelation that Being is Love"[2] and that "in the Christian's acceptance of his limitations and his involvement in time there is a depth of love and surrender which is beyond the understanding of the Stoic or the Vedantin."[3] The emphasis on surrender to divine providence also comes to the fore in Panikkar's assessment of the distinctiveness of Christianity:

> The central Christian concern is a timely reminder to Buddhism and to all the humanisms that no amount of self-effort and goodwill suffices to handle the human predicament adequately; we must remain constantly

open to unexpected and unforeseeable eruptions of Reality itself, which Christians may want to call God or divine Providence. Christianity stands for the unselfish and authentic defense of the primordial rights of Reality, of which we are not the masters.[4]

In the study and practice of both Buddhism and Christianity, Pieris finds traces of the core experience of each religion in the other so that dialogue is not a matter of encountering a completely alien religious experience and system, but rather a core-to-core meeting of the "agapeic gnosis" of Christianity and the "gnostic agape" of Buddhism.[5] On the other hand, he also emphasizes the irreducible particularity of the two religions, which itself is discovered, or rediscovered through encounter with the other. He evokes the distinctiveness of each tradition through powerful image of the "Indian sage seated in serene contemplation under the Tree of Knowledge, and the Hebrew prophet hanging painfully on the Tree of Love in a gesture of protest" as "two contrasting images that clearly situate the Buddha (the Enlightened one) and the Christ (the Anointed one) in their respective paradigmatic contexts of gnosis and agape."[6] Though *agape*, love or compassion certainly play a role in Buddhist teaching and practice, Pieris remarks that "love has no salvific value in itself, so to say, except in terms of knowledge."[7] By contrast, "Loving one's neighbor is the Christian way of knowing God. In other words, love is Christian gnosis, because one who does not love one's fellows does not know God (1 John 4:7f.) Our love for one another here in the world is the Christian *art* of knowing God."[8]

All three religious hybrids thus focus on the centrality of love and surrender as elements of Christian distinctiveness or emphasis, without denying their presence in the other religion.

2. A Hindu View of Christian Particularity

As is the case in all interpersonal and intercultural interactions, one of the most instructive or revealing paths to self-knowledge is through the other. It is indeed often through the eyes of another that one becomes most clearly aware of one's own particularity or peculiarity. So much about one's own tradition is taken for granted, or disappears in a sea of familiarity. It thus takes a stranger or an outsider to call attention to certain unique features of one's religion. The process of detecting one's own religious particularity through the eyes of religious others may shed light on both positive and negative distinctive characteristics, or reasons for not converting as well as so-called "holy envy." Though there has been much critique of Christianity by Hindu thinkers, we will focus here predominantly on those elements which have been a source of inspiration and learning, and which thus point to the distinctiveness of Christianity in relation to Hinduism.

The most famous Hindu to engage Christianity in depth is undoubtedly Mohandas Gandhi. While he had an early aversion for meat-eating and alcohol-drinking Christians, he came to read the Bible while studying in England, and was particularly impressed with the sermon on the mount, which became one of the main sources of inspiration for his life and work.[9] In addition the cross became for Gandhi "a magnet," a symbol of nonviolence and voluntary suffering:

> Though I cannot claim to be a Christian in the sectarian sense, the example of Jesus' suffering is a factor in the composition of my underlying faith in non-violence, which rules all my actions, worldly and temporal. Jesus lived and died in vain if he did not teach us to regulate the whole of life by the eternal law of love.

The importance of self-sacrificing love was thus for Gandhi a distinctive element in the experience and in the teaching of Jesus. Though Hinduism also emphasizes the role of love (*bhakti*), it is mainly as a devotional attitude toward God that it is seen as a way to salvation. Besides the "eternal law of love," Gandhi also singles out the radical forgiveness taught and exemplified by Jesus as a particular element of appeal:

> Jesus Christ prayed to God from the Cross to forgive those who had crucified him. It is my constant prayer to God that He may give me the strength to intercede even for my assassin. And it should be your prayer too that your faithful servant may be given the strength to forgive.

While Gandhi thus admired these elements in the life and teaching of Jesus, he saw no reason to convert to Christianity. Not only did he take issue with the way many Christians lived out their faith, he could not accept many of the articles of Christian faith (such as the doctrine of atonement). He also believed that each religion contained within itself resources for attaining the highest end of salvation or liberation, and that the policies of conversion had more to do with institutional power than with spiritual development.

A general aversion to conversion combined with the development of a more fundamentalist orientation in Hinduism seems to have muted the inclination of Hindu thinkers to engage Christianity in positive and constructive ways, or to pay attention to the particularity of Christianity. A notable exception to this is the Hindu scholar Anatanand Rambachan, who is one of the foremost contemporary theologians of *Advaita Vedanta*. In a recent lecture, he mentions a 1981 interreligious dialogue meeting in Rajpur, where his encounter with Christians for the first time drew his attention to the importance of justice at the center of religious consciousness.[10] He relates that his own traditional training had not engaged social questions and problems in connection to the pursuit of liberation. This encounter with Christianity, and in particular with his "favorite Christian text," (Matt. 25:31-46), led him to a critical reflection on his own tradition and a search for theological resources in the Hindu tradition that affirm the dignity of every human being and that advance social justice. This found expression in *A Hindu Theology of Liberation* in which he tackles with the problems of patriarchy, homophobia, casteism, anthropocentrism, and childism, inspired by Catholic Social Teaching but drawing from resources available in Hinduism. Like Gandhi, he also turns to the Cross as a source of inspiration. While Hinduism has many divine manifestations, none project the image of the divine "executed in pain and humiliation." The image of Jesus on the Cross is for him not only an example of non-violence (*ahimsa*), but of the depth of God's love that has no limits. *Ahimsa*, he states, is here "the outcome of love." In the case of Jesus, this love expresses itself in a special concern for the oppressed, the victims, the powerless.

For Gandhi as well as Rambachan, it is the element of Christian love expressed in terms of self-sacrifice and preferential option for the poor and the oppressed which are particularly enviable or inspiring.

3. Indian Christian Theological Reflection on Christian Particularity

As Peter Phan points out in the opening article of this volume, one of the characteristics of Christian theology in Asia is dialogue with other religious traditions. Asian theologians have indeed contributed in important ways to reflection on interreligious dialogue. Much of the theological dialogue of the past decades has focused on what Christianity can learn from other religious traditions. In light of the history of Christian triumphalism and *a priori* presumption of the radical superiority of Christianity, there has been less inclination to focus on the distinctiveness of Christian teachings and practices. Still, some Indian Christian theologians, even while embracing a more pluralist attitude toward all religions, have also ventured into reflection on the distinctiveness of Christianity in relationship to Hinduism. I will focus here in particular on the writings of George Soares-Prabhu (1929-1995) who, though lesser known beyond India, has contributed in important ways to the development of Indian Christian hermeneutics.

Soares-Prabhu starts from an open and pluralistic approach to other religions. He rejects any attempt to establish the superiority of one religion over the other as "neither practical nor wise" and celebrates the diversity of "forms of religiosity as abundantly as the flowers in a forest."[11] However, in most of his writings, he also reflects on the distinctiveness of Christianity, especially in relation to Hinduism and Buddhism. As a Biblical scholar, he focuses mainly on the experience and on the teachings of Jesus, arguing that Jesus' experience of God as unconditional love was "absolutely unique."[12] He focuses in on the particularity of the parent-child relationship, and the elements of intimacy, dependency, vulnerability, and mutual love and trust as characteristic of the Christian experience of God. He readily admits that this does not mean that Christianity has a rich set of teachings on prayer. In fact, he states that compared with Hinduism or Buddhism "prayer techniques are poorly developed in Christianity."[13] Nevertheless, he suggests that "what Jesus gives us is a new attitude in prayer, emerging out of a new experience of God."[14] Prayer is "an interpersonal 'conversation' with God, in which love is experienced and given, and relations of intimacy founded."[15]

Beyond Jesus' approach to prayer, what according to Soares-Prabhu is distinctive about Jesus' teaching is his insistence on the inseparability of love of God and love of neighbor:

It is just this intimate pairing of the love of God and the love of neighbor that constituted the specificity and the uniqueness of the teaching of Jesus. Interhuman concern is obviously an element in all religious traditions... But the interhuman concern here is always a secondary attitude which follows from a prior religious experience (liberation) or a primary commitment to God (the Covenant). It is only with Jesus that the ethical attitude becomes, as it were, an integral part of the religious experience itself, for to experience God as 'Father" is to experience the neighbor as 'brother.' The horizontal is thus inseparably welded into the vertical, and love of neighbor is brought onto a level with love of God.[16]

It is this inseparability of love of God and neighbor that represents or should represent the distinctive Christian way of being in the world. "Like the Buddhist attitude of 'mindfulness,' the Christian attitude of *agape* is thus an existential attitude derived from a change in one's being."[17] What is particular about this love is its orientation to the poor, the vulnerable and the marginalized, and its inclusion of one's enemies. Jesus' "table fellowship with sinners and outcastes" is also regarded as unique to his life and example.[18] This, of course, does not mean that Christians have themselves lived up to this example and ideal. Soares-Prabhu is particularly distressed about the fact that caste discrimination continues to exist in Christian communities in India[19] and states that "the fact that Christian *Dalits* do exist (and suffer) among us is a sign of how little Christian we are, and of how much we stand in a state of serious and, one suspects, unrepentant sin."[20]

The particularity of the Christian understanding of sin is also to be understood in relationship to its views of love since "Jesus has so radicalized the norms of right conduct (love) that all claims to sinlessness are effectively foreclosed."[21] Even as Christianity acknowledges human limitation in living up to the highest religious ideal, it also emphasizes the possibility of forgiveness as a constant and core element of Christian faith. In reflecting on what Hindus might consider to be essential and distinctive about Christianity, Soares-Prabhu states:

The Indian reader would at once identify active concern and forgiveness as the two poles, positive and negative, of the Dharma of Jesus – of that complex blend of worldview and values, of beliefs and prescriptions which 'hold together' the followers of Jesus and integrates them into a recognizable community. For if these are not exclusively Christian attitudes, the importance given to them in the teaching of Jesus and the concrete forms they assume in the New Testament give them a specifically Christian significance.[22]

This attitude of forgiveness requires "the cultivation of a non-judgmental attitude toward self and others" which has also been developed in Indian religions, from which Christians might learn.[23] However, in Christianity, forgiveness is ultimately and uniquely grounded in an all-loving and forgiving God.

In the end, for Soares-Prabhu, the uniqueness or distinctiveness of Christianity is not to be argued in theoretical or doctrinal terms, but is to be shown through a particular way of being in the world, as "the true 'uniqueness' of Christ is the uniqueness of the way of solidarity and struggle (a way that is neither male nor female) that Jesus showed as the way to life. That uniqueness cannot be argued but must be lived."[24]

Conclusion
It may seem inappropriate or risky, in light of the history of Christian triumphalism, to return to the question of the uniqueness or the particularity of Christianity. It may be regarded as a new way of asserting the superiority of Christianity in relation to other religious traditions. However, the shift from traditional conceptions of absolute uniqueness to a relational view of the particularity of Christianity may also be seen as a sign of humility, as a recognition of the specificity, but also the limits of Christianity in relation to other religious traditions. The particularity of any religion indeed points beyond itself to the particularity of the other, and to the possibility of mutual enrichment. It is in assuming one's specificity that religions might more readily live up to their own religious ideal and have something to contribute to the dialogue. The particularity or specificity of Christianity is moreover not something that is absolute and fixed, but rather something that may change depending on varying cultural and religious contexts.

While the Christian themes of love of God as inseparable from love of neighbor, sin and forgiveness come into sharp relief in the Indian religious context, this does not imply that they are absent in other Indian religions. In his lengthy discussion of redemptive love (*agape*) as distinctive of Christianity and liberating knowledge (*gnosis*) as particular to Buddhism, Aloysius Pieris also insists that "the core experience of Christianity is not *agape* pure and simple but *agape* in dialogue with *gnosis*; conversely the core experience of Buddhism is not mere *gnosis*, but a *gnosis* intrinsically in dialogue with *agape*. Hence, a true Buddhist-Christian encounter is possible only at the depths of our being where the core-to-core dialogue has already taken place!"[25]

Both orientations are thus present to various degrees in the two traditions, and dialogue then involves an awakening to an underdeveloped or less developed dimension that is latent in one's own tradition. Abhishiktananda also emphasizes that though "love of neighbor as such is scarcely directly enjoined in the Hindu Scriptures and though "Buddhist compassion cannot be identified with Christian charity," still, "the admirable examples of sacrificial service which are often met with in modern India cannot be accounted for as merely the indirect result of the preaching of the Gospel. No doubt the Gospel has acted as a vigorous reminder, a catalyst, or as a life-giving shower of rain upon the earth; but it has not come in a vacuum, and the rain has fallen upon soil which was already fertile."[26] Attention to the particularity of Christianity is thus not meant to diminish the other or to make exclusive claim to certain characteristics. It aims at acknowledging and assuming one's own highest ideals so as to contribute more effectively to the dialogue with other religions and to the common good.

Notes

1. Devaka Premawardhana, "'The Unremarkable Hybrid': Aloysius Pieris and the Redundancy of Multiple Religious Belonging" in *Journal of Ecumenical Studies* 46:1 (2011), p. 98.
2. Abhishiktananda, *Saccidananda*, London: ISPCK, 1974, p. 146.
3. *Ibid.*, p. 145.
4. Raimon Panikkar, *The Intra-Religious Dialogue*, New York: Paulist Press, 1999, p. 131.
5. Aloysius Pieris, *Love Meets Wisdom. A Christian Experience of Buddhism*, Maryknoll: Orbis, 1988, pp. 114-119.
6. Aloysius Pieris, *Love Meets Wisdom*, p. 86.
7. *Ibid.*, p. 118.
8. *Ibid.*, p. 114.
9. He did not actually regard the message of the sermon as unique to Christianity as it reminded him of a stanza he was familiar with since his youth.
10. This lecture was delivered at Boston College in October 2019 as the "Brien O'Brien and Mary

Hasten Lecture in Interreligious Dialogue." The lecture is available online.
11. *Idem.*
12. George Soares-Prabhu, *The Dharma of Jesus* (Francis D'Sa, ed.) Maryknoll: Orbis Books, 2003, p. 88.
13. *Ibid.*, p. 210. He adds that "Even the Spiritual Exercises of Ignatius of Loyola, one of the more technical treatises on prayer in the Christian tradition, would appear curiously unfinished to an Indian reader, accustomed to the meticulous instructions on diet, posture, breathing, and methods of concentration that are detailed in Indian texts on meditation." (p. 218)Abhishiktananda similarly states that "in the Gospel Jesus gave no teaching to his disciples either about methods of meditation, dhyana, or about systems of yoga. He simply commanded them to love one another." In *Saccidananda*, London: ISPCK, 1974, p. 200.
14. *Ibid.*, p. 210.
15. *Idem.*
16. *Ibid.*, p. 198.
17. *Ibid.*, p. 92. He elsewhere puts this in more contrasting terms when he states "For Jesus, the ultimate goal is not unconditional freedom (as in Hinduism and Buddhism) but unconditional love." Ibid., p. 170.
18. *Ibid.*, p. 117. Soares-Prabhu also refers to the Jewish scholar Geza Vermez who mentions this as distinctive of Jesus' life.
19. He puts it powerfully when he states that "When caste discrimination enters into the celebration of the Eucharist, the sin becomes sacrilege." *Ibid.*, p. 128.
20. *Ibid.*, p. 130.
21. *Ibid.*, p. 225.
22. *Ibid.*, p. 220.
23. "The way to self-forgivenness that would empower us to forgive others is the cultivation of a non-judgmental attitude toward ourselves and others... This will be particularly appreciated by the Indian reader, because in his tradition too non-judgmental awareness is the beginning (and the end) of wisdom and the heart of all forgiveness." *Ibid.*, pp. 224-225.
24. *Ibid.*, p. 97.
25. Aloysius Pieris, *Love Meets Wisdom*, p. 119.
26. Abhishiktananda, *Saccidananda*. London: ISPCK, 1974, p. 158.

Part Two: Inculturation of Christianity in Particular Asian Contexts

Paying Attention to Indian Tantric Buddhism

THIERRY-MARIE COURAU

Indian tantric Buddhism spread throughout Asia during the second half of the first millennium of our era following the preceding Indian Buddhist trends. It has an essential place, often unrecognised, among the foundations of its religious cultures and traditions. Visible signs of this are representations of mandalas *and* bodhisattvas. *It forms part of the current of the Great Vehicle, within which it offers spiritual practices that are paradoxical given the origins of Buddhism. The churches owe it to themselves to engage with this field of research if they want to continue developing a better understanding of Asian cultures in terms of their roots, discover in them how God reveals in them his relation to human beings, and allow themselves to be transformed by this encounter.*

Not remaining outside worlds, which welcome it and to which it belongs from now on, in order to make itself ever more available for encounters in order to let people discover the One by whom it lives, this is part of the fundamental structure of Christianity. Since its mental universe was formatted by the West, it has a duty to take itself beyond this base and move into the cultures that form the soil in which it has recently found itself. It has a responsibility to listen to them in an effort to grow in understanding of them, dialogue with them and understand itself better. It is in this way that it learns to see how God has always given himself to them and how he wants to give himself to the world today.

The great diversity of Asian cultures was produced by the absorption of many influences. Among these I think it is important to stress the importance of significant elements of the vision of Indian tantric Buddhism. They are part of the foundations of their cultural, spiritual and religious systems, whether Buddhist or not, and whether the elements are recognised for what they are or not.

Indian tantric Buddhism in Asia
The spread of Indian Buddhism

India and its religions have spread beyond the Indian sub-continent, over an area that can be described in broad terms as from Afghanistan in the west to Japan in the east, and from Mongolia in the north to Indonesia in the south.

Before they arrived in their tantric form, Indian doctrines and practices were spread from the beginning of our era by the journeys of Indian merchants, both by land and sea. The strength of their religious systems supported political and economic centres, sometimes giving them their permanent structure and affecting the mass of the populations down to today.[1] In this way Buddhism developed by creating lasting structures, grafting itself on to local cultures, creating variants that formed hybrids between each other and interacted between geographical areas, albeit unequally in history.

Without losing anything of its original inspiration, Indian Buddhism evolved considerable during the first fifteen centuries of its existence. Its tantric forms, appearing from the 4th to 5th centuries onwards, are both the sign of its final completion and its brand. This last stage of the spread of Buddhism, from tantric India, integrates the previous layers that, as it were, prepared and tilled the ground in which this form implanted itself for the long term.[2] Schools that had developed before the arrival of tantrism (a Western neologism coined from the Sanskrit *tantra*, used to indicate texts) would have greater or less difficulty in continuing to exist alongside it. Alternatively, they might regain force, reject it later and reinvent themselves, sometimes for reasons that were political rather than religious. Whatever their situation, they were influenced by tantrism to the point of including in their doctrines and practices some aspects that were sometimes contradictory. This was so widespread that, almost everywhere in Asia, we can find signs of it, including on lands marked by the arrival of Islam and Christianity.[3]

Paying Attention to Indian Tantric Buddhism

The Asian exoteric visibility of an esoteric Indian tradition
Indian tantric Buddhism is called esoteric. Local Asian spiritual traditions, native or already the product of an earlier encounter with the Buddhist world, whether esoteric or not, echoed or hybridised with the earlier form and produced unique complex esoteric systems. The best-known examples are Chinese, Tibetan and Nepalese Buddhism. Others are Chinese religious traditions like Taoism. Research carried out for over twenty years helps us to understand this interaction better.

The exoteric, visible dimension of esoteric Indian tantrism will be familiar even if they do not use the term. Through architecture first of all. Stone *mandalas* form part of the most beautiful and most important monuments in the history of the planet: Boroboduret Prabanam on the island of Java (Indonesia), Angkor (Cambodia), the Forbidden City of Beijing (China) or of Hué (Vietnam).

If the *mandala* is one powerful symbolic representation that marks the presence of the tantric Indian world, a religious figure is another powerful symbol of it, *Guanyin*.[4] Familiar in Taiwan, she may seem Chinese, and is in many ways, before having been adopted in Korea and Japan, and also in Vietnam, for example. She then spread throughout the world. Nevertheless she was born in Indian Buddhism. *Guanyin* is one of the Chinese names of the *bodhisattva* of compassion known in India by the Sanskrit name of *Avalokiteshvara*.[5]

This *bodhisattva* has occupied considerable space in the Buddhism of the Great Vehicle from the beginning of our era, as shown by the spread of its images, texts and doctrines throughout Asia, depending on periods and places. One of the most famous tantric representations comes from the *sûtra of dhâranî,* 'the great compassion, vast and overcoming all obstacles, of the *bodhisattva,* who contemplates the world with a thousand hands and a thousand eyes'.[6] In this short Indian tantric text (perhaps 7th century), the *bodhisattva Avalokiteshvara* teaches a formula in Sanskrit called a *dhâranî* ('which carries memory'). By reciting this invocation, the faithful know they are saved. The *bodhisattva's* limitless compassion that allows them to see the sufferings of creatures and come to their aid is symbolised by their thousand hands and thousand eyes. Elsewhere it may be endowed with eleven or twenty-seven faces, or represented with different numbers of arms. Its images are innumerable and so are the reasons for invoking it in various versions of Buddhism.[7] The followers of Japanese Zen Buddhism recite this tantric *dhâranî* every day. As for the Dalai Lama, that eminent figure of Tibetan tantric Buddhism, he is regarded, like all other Tibetan sovereigns, an earthly emanation of this *bodhisattva*.

Indian tantric Buddhism and its fundamentals
The importance of the exoteric aspects of Indian tantric Buddhism in Asia allows us to measure the strength of its foundations. In the world of Asian culture the totality of its dimensions, doctrinal, moral, and social, forms a set of resources, recognised or unrecognised, explicit or implicit, that enable us to appreciate the way to approach the world and society, religion, life and death.

The figure of the *bodhisattva Guanyin* is a good entry point. Several centuries after the death of the historic Buddha, Gautama (5th century BCE), there developed the concept of the *bodhisattvas*, beings striving for Awakening. This marks the development of the main family of Buddhist traditions, known as the Great Vehicle. These individuals, in the higher stages, may acquire the qualities of the Buddha's Awakening while resolving not to leave living creatures definitively, because of a vow they made at the beginning of their journey that binds them to living creatures. Any individual can make this commitment to attain awakening for the good of others, for their deliverance, in the presence of an awakened being. They renounce the possibility of leaving the flux of existences as long as there are beings wandering in it. To advance along the path of liberation they have no need to become a renouncer of the world, a celibate or mendicant, devoting themselves exclusively to a spiritual discipline within a group of solitaries and in accordance with their rule. This differentiates these people from the followers of the 'senior' traditions, who reject this evolution and claim to observe the original precepts of the historical Buddha, for example, the Theravada school. The question of renunciation changes register. It is no longer connected with the fact of acting in, with and for the world, but in a manner not favourable to Awakening. It is while being active in society that the *bodhisattva*, master of the house or not, chooses to renounce subjection to the action of poisons such as greed for acquisition, aversion and blindness, and to journey gradually until they reach the liberating knowledge with and for all.

The Great Vehicle: new doctrinal perspectives

New texts (*sūtra* and treatises) and novel figures of awakened beings accompanied this development of Buddhism, which takes the name of the Vehicle of the *bodhisattva*, and is also known as the Great Vehicle (*Mahāyāna*). Unprecedented doctrinal approaches justified this evolution by claiming it to be the only position able to expose all the obstacles that the spirit constantly recreates for itself on the road that should be leading it to total liberation. The Madhyamaka school - with the emblematic figure of Nāgārjuna (2nd century CE) – is the model. It adopts the approach of walking 'in the middle', on a ridge as narrow as a two-edged sword, sharpened and cutting off all support. All beings, all things, are empty of any existence of their own – including this proposition! This is so much so that anyone who would have thought they had reached and understood emptiness to grasp it for security on the path to knowledge and deliverance would be further from them than the stupid person wallowing in the passions of the flesh.

Another thesis comes to challenge that of Madhyamaka: Vijñānavāda. Asaṅga, who, with his brother Vasubandhu (4th-5th centuries CE), is said to be the author of this, emphasises a very structured presentation of forms of discernment or knowledge (*vijñāna*), which are the foundation of the experiences of the spirit that are responsible for the appearance and disappearance of worlds. The brothers offer answers to the debate that runs through Buddhism and the other Indian traditions about the flux of existences *(saṃsāra)*.

In an Indian world in search of spiritual solutions, the Buddhist way also envisages other doctrinal approaches based on the one hand on the interpenetration of microcosmoses and microcosmoses and on the other on the idea that each individual carries within them a Buddha seed, a seed that makes them a potential Buddha. This is the source of the idea that there is a Buddha nature in each being, which is the origin of religious innovations from which tantric or Sinicised Buddhist Asia have drawn great benefit.

A new stage with durable effects: tantrism

Tantric elements within Indian Great Vehicle Buddhism have been identified by researchers from as early as the 4th and 5th centuries CE, even before they became visible within the Hindu world or formed a complete system of teaching, probably towards the end of the 7th century. First a strictly Indian complex system with various ramifications appears in the Himalayan region of the north, the product of groups of transgressive ascetics. Then it evolves and becomes richer as it spreads over the whole of the sub-continent and comes into contact with earlier religious traditions, which it transforms. In the end it forms a complex of religious and social experiences, corpuses of texts, specific figures and practices that are very original. Within this globalising understanding of the universe, in which cosmic forces, human and superhuman, interpenetrate and act with each other, with the faithful playing an active role, yogic practices very naturally find their place and spread. They are inseparable from the system because of the importance of the body in the *tantra*.[8]

The tantric perspective on Buddhism belongs to the development of the Great Vehicle and its perspectives. Its particularity within the history of Buddhism is due less to the essence of its doctrine and its aims than to its methods, which rely on specific texts *(tantra)*, physical *(hathayoga)* and ascetic exercises, formulas *(mantra)*, actions, symbolic representations, drawn, painted – like the *yantra* (the symbolic support), sculpted or built, which associate numerous deities to ritual areas. In all this the *mantra* plays a key role. Rituals, which are essential and form part of the methods, associate music, smells, food, dance, sophisticated clothes and hairstyles, fire, actors, gestures and movements, combined or not, collective forms, forms for two people or individual forms. This world of colour and sound, with vibrant and diverse energies, introduces us into a sphere beyond the devotee's normal state and vision, and enables them to penetrate or recognise the world of the 'gods' and their qualities.

The general principle that guides Buddhist tantric action is participation in the life of a deity in his or her palace and in identifying them mentally or through representations. A deity is a powerful symbolic element of the system of doctrine and practice that is one way of enabling the participant to recognise the interplay of passions and forms of wisdom. The deity is an image of the Awakening the *yogin* seeks to discover in themselves and in the cosmos. Through a process of generation of a deity and then completion, the participant has the experience of being put in touch with the nature of their spirit and its primordial qualities. In Tibet the iconography of deities sexually united, called *enyab-yum* (father-mother), of the tantra of the supreme yoga (*anuttarayogatantra*), represents the understanding (*prajñā*) or knowledge, generally a feminine attribute, united with compassion (*karuṇā*), skilful techniques (*upāyakauśalya*), and method, a masculine attribute.

Tantric practice of the Buddhist great Vehicle is reputed to be the practice of a very rapid path to attaining Awakening, liberation, in one existence. This speed is accessible only to devotees who have already followed an extremely serious and fruitful path in the two previous successive levels of advancement (*yāna*) known as the 'lower' (*hīna*) and the 'higher' (*mahā*). Practice in the last, lightning (*vajira*) level can only be carried out in a close relation between a master and experienced disciples, which is what gives it its esoteric dimension. It is only these disciples that are introduced into the secrets of the texts and the exercises, which have to be interpreted to be passed on and practised correctly, without danger. Ordinary devotees or practitioners, who make up the majority of followers of a Buddhist school, share its tantric 'atmosphere' through its public activities and its ritual and artistic representations. Although they cannot reach the ultimate, definitive meaning of what they see, hear and feel – which is the liberating knowledge that is the aim of the practice – they receive, from their preliminary practices, even if these are cursory, benefits that enable them to live better their everyday lives and their spiritual lives. In this way they develop their devotion for the path and become familiar with it with a view to going on, during this existence or another, to the subsequent stages that will gradually open up for them the highest levels of the method. Gradualism is inherent in the Buddhist offer of liberation.

In a paradoxical, or even shocking, way, tantric Buddhist paths may include elements that are despised, or even rejected or forbidden, in the old Buddhist traditions that relied particularly on the instructions of the historical Buddha. Endowed by the *tantra* with a 'spiritual utility', these elements are used in the master-disciple relationship as useful means for those who can benefit from them with a view to liberation at the stage they have reached. This potentiality is not a feature of these instruments in themselves. It concerns, for example, mantras, sacrificial rituals, fire sacrifice, symbolic representations, instruments, amulets, the use of meat or fish as food, of alcohol; psychic creations, visualisations; the use and value of magical powers developed by practices of training the mind and bodily, physical practices (*hathayoga, prāṇāyāma,* etc.); engaging in sexual relations; dreams and divination, etc. In this way Indian, and later Asian, Buddhism produced a sophisticated method in an astonishing way, even if at first sight it seems in total contradiction with the original idea and its practical applications. This coherent system, the result of a close association between practices and theories, takes note of all the apparent contradictions and intensifies them in an attempt to resolve them by means of a change in the way people see the nature of reality.

The success of the Buddhist tantric path does not lie in a change of objective in relation to the original Buddhism, whose fundamental teaching is expressed in the Four Truths of the Noble Ones. Its particularity resides in the combination of 'knowledge' with 'skilful means', as the Great Vehicle envisages. This allows the yogi to reach the desired objective – recognising the state of Awakening from which the devotee has never been separated, the primordial unity of their spirit.

Choosing to occupy a decisive area
A light opening on to the mystery of God and human beings
Asian cultures have a vocation to enter into dialogue with the whole of the planet, and they have already done so, more or less sporadically or intensely depending on the particular culture. For fifty years the impact of Indian yoga, Tibetan or Japanese Buddhism, Chinese practices with regard to energy, is undeniable in Western environments and beyond. All the same, while a Westerner may have the impression of knowing them through the practices to which they have given rise, India, Tibet, Japan and China remain hermetically closed to Westerners. A Westerner's approach is often predatory towards them.

Indian tantric Buddhism, associated with many clichés, as seductive as they are repulsive, is not the only entrance, nor even the most accessible, but it offers this particularity of being a feature shared with and inspirational in many aspects of Asian religious, cultural and social life. To take one example, I should like to stress how much, together with the lineages that have come from it, it teaches us particularly the importance of emotions and passions in human life, and of attempts to give them meaning. It goes even further in making them instruments that help to free us from attitudes that are mistaken, painful and cause suffering. It cannot be an accident that the Asian world as a whole has been heavily impacted by this form of Buddhism and has absorbed it, in one way or another, into its practices and traditions. Sometimes it may even have done this in a utilitarian way or in contradiction to its liberationist aims. But in this case too, its use emphasises the attention that should be given to the psycho-physical human energies, which are themselves in relation with the energies of the universe.

The lesson of tantric Buddhism thus invites us to be aware of the distinction that must be made between the psychic confusion and clarity within which emotions are expressed. By the range of obstacles it places on the path of the emotions, confusion simply increases the emotional pressure at work, and multiplies its unfavourable consequences for the balance of a person's inner and relational psychic life. In contrast, clarity, when it accompanies the emotions, makes it possible for their energies to be released in security and confidence, like a river, whose different historical beds have been respected, so that when there is an exceptional inflow of water, they can channel it to the sea without damage.

For the incarnation tradition represented by Christianity, this allowance for emotional life is key. From many points of view, Christianity has neglected it or relegated it to a marginal role. It has adopted a long-term position of ignoring its value to people's personal and relational equilibrium. Encountering a different approach that existed in Asia before the arrival of Christianity is an opportunity for Christianity to receive a new light for its understanding of the mystery of human beings and God.

A narrative theological approach combining anthropology and archaeology
Envisaging this tantric perspective, while it is neither necessarily apparent nor obvious, is like an archaeological approach. Really listening to the world of Asia today means entering into its intimate history, the dimension that does not appear at first sight. The archaeological perspective means working with memory, in the layers and interactions of history, and not simply from the context, which is no more than an opaque display window. When we dig into memory, we find the threads and the weave of the fabric that go to form the context. Access to this memory is attained by combining disciplines and specialisms, and requires time and distance. It

does not provide an exact reconstruction of the history of individuals, their ideas and their practices, the worlds they inhabited or passed through, but the possibility of telling stories, constructing narratives that speak today to those who are their heirs. These narratives take account of the depth, the beauty and the complexity of human relations without taboos, their sensibility and their emotion. This memory is a present, the present borne by those to whom it belongs. In it there is revealed a creative potential, buried resources, forgotten treasures, not only for those who carried them, but also for everyone else.

This archaeological theological study is not seeking knowledge in the same way as religious studies but tries to understand the density of human experience. It may analyse, but it does not seek so much to explain as to gain acquaintance. Beyond any doubt, in it we see the way God has structured his encounter with human beings since the beginning.

By outlining rapidly and very generally the foundations of an intrinsic characteristic of the spiritual life of Asian cultures, which first emerged in India and then spread everywhere, in different ways from the other great religious traditions such as Christianity or Islam, I want to encourage all of us who are Christian theologians, whether Asian or not, to get involved in this area of research.[9] Some people have already ventured into the area, but not many. We need within the churches a research institution focused on Indian tantric Buddhism that seeks to understand its history and the roots it has sunk in Asia, the same task, perhaps, that the Cairo-based Dominican Institute for Oriental Studies (IDEO) performs for Arab and Muslim literature.

Translated by Francis McDonagh

Notes

1. Ronald M Davidson, *Indian Esoteric Buddhism*, New York, 2002.
2. Andrea Acri, *Esoteric Buddhism in Mediaeval Maritime Asia: Networks of Masters, Texts, Icons*, Singapore, 2016.
3. Laszlo Legeza, 'Tantric Elements in Pre-Hispanic Philippines Gold Art', *Arts of Asia*, July–August 1988, 129–136.
4. Michel Strickmann, *Mantras et mandarins: Le bouddhisme tantrique en Chine*, Paris, 1996.
5. Louis Frédéric, *Les dieux du bouddhisme: Guide iconographique*, Paris, 1992.
6. *Senjusengenkanzeonbosatsukôdaienman muge daihishindaranikyô*, Taishô XX, 1060.
7. *Le Bouddha de compassion. Images de Guanyin*, traduit du chinois par Wang Guo-Qing, Gap

(France), 2007. Original edition: Taipei (Taiwan), 2000.
8. André Padoux, *L'énergie de la parole dans les textes tantriques*, Paris, 1965; *Comprendre le tantrisme. Les sources hindoues*, Paris, 2010; *The Hindu Tantric World. An Overview*, Chicago, Ill., 2017.
9. David Gordon White (ed.), *Tantra in Practice*, Princeton, NJ, 2000.

A Metaphysical Approach to Theology in Taiwan: Dialogues between Catholicism and Daoist Teachings of Laozi and Zhuangzi

KATIA LENEHAN

This article focuses on revealing, from the perspective of metaphysics, different integration approaches in dialogues between Catholicism and Daoist philosophy adopted in Catholic studies in Taiwan. Three Taiwanese philosophers (as well as theologians) are included. Each one represents a particular way to approach the relationship between Catholicism and Daoism. Through a comparative approach we are able to see a valuable fusion of Catholicism and Daoist philosophy. And hopefully, these different methods will shed a light on the inculturation of Catholic thought in Asia.

I. Introduction

Since Matteo Ricci's (1552-1610) visit to China, most researchers have paid special attention to the dialogue between and integration of Catholic philosophy and Confucianism. On the whole, during the process of inculturation of Catholicism, the emphasis on Daoist philosophy has not been as prominent as that of Confucianism (Daoism here refers to the Daoist teaching of the Pre-Qin period, and the organized Daoist religious institutions formed after the Han Dynasty are not included in the discussion of this article). However, the metaphysics implied in Daoism and its implications for theology issues are of great significance for Christianity in Asia. In particular, the achievements of Daoism in the area of metaphysics have obviously surpassed Confucianism, which focuses more on human ethics.

This article will attempt to sort out and reveal, from the perspective of metaphysics, different approaches to the integration of Catholicism and Daoist philosophy adopted in previous studies. Three Taiwanese philosophers (as well as theologians) are included. Each one represents a particular way to approach the relationship between Catholicism and Daoism. And hopefully, these different methods will shed a light on a more in-depth reflection on the localization of Catholic thought.

II. Archbishop Stanislaus Lo Kuang: Dao in the universe is in no way identical with God who can be both in and beyond the universe

Lo Kuang (1911-2004) conducted a very in-depth study of Chinese philosophy. He argued that China does not have a religious philosophy in the Western sense, since Chinese philosophy as a whole is actually a philosophy of life. "Chinese philosophers do not discuss religious beliefs, because Chinese philosophy, as a philosophy of life, only discusses things within the universe, and does not discuss things beyond the universe."[1] That said, Chinese philosophy's emphasis on life does not mean that the Chinese are without religious beliefs, because in the process of life, as Lo Kuang claims, man will be naturally involved with religious beliefs.

Accordingly, Dao falls under the domain of the universe while God extends beyond the universe. As a result, although Chinese philosophers believe in God, God is not within the scope of the study of Chinese philosophy. Lo believes that when Laozi depicts Dao as something indescribable or even unnamable, he in fact recognizes a transcendent quality of Dao; however, this is only an epistemological transcendence rather than an ontological one. As Lo put it, "Dao possesses a transcendent quality epistemologically, but not ontologically, this is because Dao transforms itself and produces all things, it dwells therefore only in all things. God, however, is transcendent both epistemologically and ontologically."[2]

In this way, Lo argued that although the Chinese regard Dao as an absolute substance, this substance is merely within the universe. It is "not a transcendent substance [beyond the universe], but merely an infinite substance [in the universe]."[3] Furthermore, Lo mentioned that Laozi's claim "Dao produces all things" shows that Dao also has the power of creation, but this power is in no way God's power to create out of nothing.

If so, what would this mean in Laozi's statement "the myriad things of the world are born of being; being is born of nonbeing"?[4] Lo asserts that "non-being" characterizes merely Dao's quality of "indefinite," or "intangible." The quotation simply illustrates how creatures evolve from the indefinite to the definite, from the indeterminate to the determinate, or, from vagueness to the concrete, which is in essence different from God's creation from nothing.[5]

In short, although Lo admits that Dao is an infinite substance, yet to him it is a substance that exists only within the confines of the universe. And most important of all, Dao is "a distant and vague substance, an impersonal substance, which is different from a loving God."[6]

In addition, ultimate transcendence in human life in Daoism is to be united with Dao. One finds that the core of being is Dao, so one forgets oneself and all things in order to become one with Dao, and from the perspective of Dao, one is able to view all things in the universe as equal. Nevertheless, when becoming one with Dao, Lo declares, the person disappears, and only Dao remains, which is obviously different from transcendence in Catholicism, since the union between man and God does not lead to an ontological mixture of both.[7] Lo's statement seems to imply that Laozi and Zhuangzi's teachings are inclined towards the trappings of pantheism.

III. Gabriel Chen-Ying Ly: Dao belongs to the realm of principle while God to the realm of reality

In his nine-volume series of *Man and God: A Probe into Chinese and Western Atheism*, Chen-Ying Ly (1929-) includes a very detailed discussion on Dao. In the fourth volume, he reflects on Dao in the context of the tension between immanence and transcendence. Ly has a comprehensive yet deep understanding of the tendency towards immanence in Chinese philosophy. He finds that the religious experience of Chinese people often starts from within with personal experience and follows with a search for connection with the transcendent. Based on this connection, one is able to proceed from the finite to the infinite, from the secular to the holy.

Ly points out that Dao itself in *Laozi and Zhuangzi* has the quality of fundamentality, immanence, and pervasiveness. "Fundamentality" demonstrates the root or pole all things come from. Laozi says, "Dao produces them [all things]. Virtue raises them."⁸ Therefore, "virtue" is the differentiation of Dao and lies within people and things. In short, as "virtue" originated from Dao, things gain their own natures. In this regard, Dao exists in the form of "virtue" within all things, but at the same time is the origin that transcends all things. Dao is therefore "immanent in and transcendent to all things."⁹ This is why the Dao is said to possess the quality of "immanence." Also, since Dao exists in all things and "is working in all things without any constraints,"¹⁰ it can be said to have the quality of "pervasiveness."

Starting from the tension between immanence and transcendence, Ly shows two kinds of transcendence of Dao: the horizontal and the vertical. Horizontal transcendence comes from Dao's circumstantial and ubiquitous characteristics. The reason why Dao can pervade all things is precisely because all things in the universe, including heaven, earth and humans, all come from Dao and are made of it. This reveals that Dao is the origin and the cause of all things, and this also confirms Dao's pre-existence, otherwise it cannot be the cause of all things. In this regard, Ly offered a most insightful insight, indicating that there is no contradiction between the pre-existence of Dao and the pre-existence of God:

> This pre-existence of Dao is obviously a metaphysical, logical one. It is by no means referring to the order of time. Since Dao itself is universal, immanent in all things yet not constrained by them, it is of course conceptual and belongs to the realm of principles, even though it exists in the real world and is based on the reality. As the principle, it is extremely abstract, yet real; it is absolutely universal, yet involving each concrete thing…The reason why Dao is Dao is that without it, nothing can exist. So, if God is not made according to Dao, he cannot be God. The focus we should pay attention to here is that there is no contradiction between the pre-existence of Dao and the pre-existence of God, because the pre-existence here is viewed from two different perspectives: the pre-existence of Dao is conceptual and logical while God's pre-existence is of reality. God is the truth of everything and as well the final cause of human cognition. In other words, if the root of inner structure of all things is Dao, which is the most fundamental factor in the realization of all things, this whole thing must be determined by God.¹¹

In Ly's understanding, Dao is simply a concept which belongs to the realm of the principle, construing the fundamental rule of all things in reality. It therefore cannot be called "an infinite substance," since its infiniteness implies only "unlimited" or "indefinable," which is completely distinguishable from the infinity of divine substance.[12] That said, for Ly, the realm of principle and the realm of reality are not contradictory to one another. On the contrary, the two can be and should be very well combined, and this can be clearly seen from the vertical transcendence of Dao.

This so-called vertical transcendence of Dao demonstrates that Dao is not only open to humans and all things on Earth, but also to the divine or to Heaven, forming a vertical ascent of Dao. If Dao is enclosed in humanity or constrained on Earth, the integrity and completeness of Dao would be damaged, and it would thereby no longer be Dao.[13] Ly therefore argues that although Laozi and Zhuangzi do not focus on the divinity of Heaven, they still have to confirm that there is a divine as real Absolute above man and Earth, otherwise the spiritual freedom in their teaching is nothing more than a reflection of man's empty wishes or yearnings, and Zhuangzi's "wandering with the Creator"[14] is then of no substantial meaning whatsoever. In a nutshell, when the Dao of Laozi and Zhuangzi is leading towards a divine Dao of Heaven, then this Dao and the Absolute Other are literally one.

It is worth noting that although human beings can gradually ascend and merge with Dao by their inherent "virtues", Ly claims that they do not thereby become Dao. Becoming one with Dao indicates only the inner connection or inner unity between Dao and Man, but this does not obliterate the real distinction between the two. "For this reason, Zhuangzi's philosophy may be full of mysticism, it does not make him fall into the predicament of pantheism."[15]

IV. Vincent Shen: Dao is an impersonal ultimate reality while God is a personal ultimate reality as well as an ultimate Other

Vincent Shen (1949-2018) provides a very detailed analysis of the Dao of Daoism. In addition to definitions of the "way" and the "speech", he believes Dao has three philosophical meanings: (1) Dao is the law of changes, such as exchanges or a back and forth between being and non-being, movement and stillness, *yin* and *yang*, rigid and soft. In short, it is the law of change of all things in the universe. In this regard, Vincent Shen thinks that Heaven (or the Dao of Heaven) is similar to today's natural law, referring simply to its cosmological signification. From this perspective, Vincent Shen's understanding of Dao is different from Ly's, since Ly regards the Dao of Heaven as a principle open to the "divine" transcendent. (2) Regarding the birth of the universe, Dao is the source of energy: "Dao produces one. One produces two. Two produce three. Three produce myriad things."[16] This process is that of the manifestation and differentiation of Dao, a process distinguished from the creation out of nothing (*creatio ex nihilo*) in Western theology. (3) Dao refers to endless existential activity itself: Dao is not the being of beings as Heidegger said, but an ultimate reality. It is not only the law of change followed by all things, nor is it only the root that can give birth to all things. It is endless existential activity itself. A personal God is thus divinity manifested by Dao in reality.[17]

The third meaning is crucial. It has acted as a springboard for a new research perspective differing from that of Lo Kuang and Chen-Ying Ly. This new perspective does not confine Dao within the universe as Lo suggests, nor does it confine Dao to the realm of principles as Ly states. Shen claims that Dao itself is also an ultimate reality, presenting itself as endless existential activity. If Dao is an ultimate reality, it then can extend beyond the universe as well as beyond the realm of principles. In other words, all the confinements proposed by Lo and Ly are no longer tenable.

However, Dao and God are not identical. Shen clearly claims that "Dao is an undivided state before the differentiation of all things, even before the differentiation of Heaven and Earth. In this regard, Dao is endless existential activity itself, other than a "substance". Dao therefore is a non-substantial and impersonal ultimate reality, which is distinguished from the concept of personal God and from the first Substance proposed by Thomas Aquinas."[18]

But the problem arises when we recognize Dao as an ultimate reality, the root of all things yet impersonal and substantial, because Dao in this way is transcendent both cognitively and ontologically, and this will result in a dilemma: given that God and Dao are both ultimate reality, if I accept a personal and substantive ultimate reality—God, do I necessarily reject an impersonal and non-substantive ultimate reality that Laozi and Zhuangzi have experienced? Or conversely, if I accept the impersonal and intangible Dao, do I then have to reject God?

The new direction adopted by Shen suggests a complementarity between Chinese and Western thinking. He proclaims that there may exist a tension between the personal and the impersonal with regard to an ultimate reality, but that the two are not in conflict. Moreover, even if God is personal, he is not a person that can be conceived of from a human perspective. Based on a saying of Yves Raguin, S.J. (1912-1998), Shen emphasizes that God is super personal. "Although God is personal, he has also an impersonal aspect. For example, God governs the universe with his eternal laws, and these laws are completely impersonal. For this reason, he [Yves Raguin] claims that God is super personal."[19]

In addition, Shen observes that ultimate reality in Buddhism and in Daoism both possess an impersonal tendency. In this light, Shen suggests a significant distinction between ultimate reality and ultimate Other. "All major religions as well as most systems of philosophy affirm the existence of the ultimate reality, but it is not necessarily an ultimate Other."[20] God is not only an ultimate reality but also an ultimate Other. Insofar as a human subject tends to be self-enclosed, a thinking and loving ultimate Other conduces one to go out of oneself towards others and avoid being trapped in self-enclosure. Shen also perceives that Chinese philosophy emphasizes the inner connection between man and ultimate reality, so one must start from (or base oneself on) this inner (immanent) experience in order to move towards ultimate reality. The impersonal ultimate reality described in Daoism and in Buddhism may well promote one's spiritual freedom, however, "is this freedom itself ultimate or not? If this inner freedom is ultimate, one is likely to again fall into self-enclosure." On top of that, Shen warns that "the over-emphasis on impersonality [of ultimate reality] will make one left in an obscure state or realm full of nameless laws."[21] Briefly speaking, based on a Christian understanding of ultimate reality (God), Shen pinpoints the possible crises caused by over-emphasizing an impersonal ultimate reality.

Shen rejects the idea that Daoism is pantheist. He indicates that although Dao is the root of all things, it is "not completely homogeneous" in them and that there exist a tension between Dao and all things, a tension shown as "different yet complementary, continuous yet interrupted."[22]

V. Conclusion

The dialogue between Christian monotheism and Daoist metaphysics has opened up a deep theological reflection, which involves issues concerning the creation or origin of the universe, the immanence and transcendence of human beings, the personality of ultimate reality, as well as the question of pantheism and non-pantheism.

Lo Kuang, Chen-Ying Ly, and Vincent Shen follow the philosophical systems from Aristotle to Aquinas. However, when treating the dialogue between Christianity and Daoism, they develop three different approaches. Lo takes an approach of surpassing, placing Dao within the world of life and of changes, or, within the universe, while God in faith and his creation out of nothing are above and beyond the universe; the fusion of Christianity and Daoism is thus somewhat similar to the combination of the above and the below, the sacred and the secular. Ly adopts a method of absorption and integration. The combination of God and Dao no longer has the distinction between the upper and the lower, the sacred and the secular, but the distinction between the reality and the principle or rationale; in this light, Christian thought and Daoism are, to a certain extent, blended together in a more equal way. Differing from Lo and Ly, Shen's view is closer to a model of religious dialogue in the context of multiculturalism and globalization. He is not only committed to conversation and integration between cultures, but is also committed to an approach that enables different cultures/religions to enrich and complement one another. Shen states, "The reason why religious conversation is possible, as far as religious philosophy and metaphysics is concerned, is that there exist multiple views on the divine ultimate reality."[23] For him, the impersonal and non-substantial manner displayed by Dao is also one of the forms of ultimate reality. Based on this, he argues that God in Christianity also has a super personal aspect with a view to unfold a possibility of alternative revelations of God other than that of a personal God. Furthermore, Shen also notices that the impersonal Dao falls short when serving as the ultimate basis for human immanence, so he upholds the indispensability and importance of an ultimate Other who can think and love, a God revealed in Catholic faith. As a result, Christianity and Daoism to some extent achieve mutual enrichment and complementation by way of reaching for a common ground, yet reserving respective uniqueness.

Finally, on the problem of pantheism caused by Daoism due to the ubiquitous nature of Dao, Lo suspects that Daoism risks a tendency towards pantheism while Ly and Shen reject this view and offer clarifications. The way in which Dao is in all things is similar to the way in which the cause is presented in its effect. Dao does not make all things lose themselves. It can be analogized with the Christian statement that all things are in God. Without a pantheistic tendency, Daoism is closer to the "pan-en-theism" that Fr. Aloysius B. Chang, S. J. (1929-2015) and Chan Tak-kwong detect.[24]

Notes

1. Lo Kuang, *A Comparative Research between Chinese and Western Religious Philosophies*, Taipei: Central Cultural Relics Supply, 1982, 256.
2. Lo Kuang, *A Comparative Research between Chinese and Western Religious Philosophies*, 260.
3. Lo Kuang, *A Comparative Research between Chinese and Western Religious Philosophies*, 206.
4. Laozi, *Tao Te Ching*, trans. by Derek Lin, Woodstock: Sky Light Paths Pub., c2006, 81.
5. Lo Kuang, *A Comparative Research between Chinese and Western Religious Philosophies*, 206.
6. Lo Kuang, *Metaphysics of Life*, Taipei: Student Book, 2001, 378.
7. Lo Kuang, *Metaphysics of Life*, 346, 371.
8. Laozi, *Tao Te Ching*, 103.
9. Chen-Ying Ly, *Man and God: A Probe into Chinese and Western Atheism*, Vol. 4, New Taipei City: Fu Jen Catholic University Press, 1994, 27.
10. Chen-Ying Ly, *Man and God: A Probe into Chinese and Western Atheism*, Vol. 4, 37.
11. Chen-Ying Ly, *Man and God: A Probe into Chinese and Western Atheism*, Vol. 4, 39-40.
12. Chen-Ying Ly, *Man and God: A Probe into Chinese and Western Atheism*, Vol. 4, 64.
13. Chen-Ying Ly, *Man and God: A Probe into Chinese and Western Atheism*, Vol. 4, 71.
14. Chuang tzu, *The Complete Works of Chuang tzu*, trans. by Burton Watson, NY: Colombia University Press, 1968, 373. In the last two decades, the spelling "Zhuangzi" in Chinese pinyin has been wildly accepted, therefore in the main text I use "Zhuangzi" while in the footnotes the name "Chuang tzu" remains as printed in the earlier translation work.
15. Chen-Ying Ly, *Man and God: A Probe into Chinese and Western Atheism*, Vol. 4, 85.
16. Laozi, *Tao Te Ching*, 85.
17. Vincent Shen, *Metaphysics*, Taipei: National Taiwan University Press, 2019, 64-65.
18. Vincent Shen, *Metaphysics*, 65.
19. Vincent Shen, *Metaphysics*, 250.
20. Vincent Shen, *Contrast, Strangification, and Dialogues*, Taipei: Wunan Books, 2013, 523.
21. Vincent Shen, *Metaphysics*, 252.
22. Vincent Shen, *Metaphysics*, 40.
23. Vincent Shen, *Metaphysics*, 253.
24. Aloysius B. Chang, *My Humble Opinion on Chinese Spiritual Practice*, Taipei: Kuangchi Culture Group, 1978, 142-145. Also see Chan Tak-kwong, 'Taiwan Scholastic Philosophy: Mysticism', in Katia Lenehan (ed.), *The Theoretical Development of Taiwan Scholastic Philosophy*, New Taipei City: Fu Jen Catholic university Press, 2015, 175.

Productive Imagination in the Story Theology of Choan-Seng Song[1]

YA-TANG CHUANG

Story theology, proposed and developed by Choan-Seng Song, played an important role in doing theology in Asia. In this paper, the author tries, by grafting to analysis of imagination in the philosophical hermeneutics of Paul Ricoeur, to investigate the secret power hidden in story theology. Intertextuality, one of presuppositions of productive imagination maintained by Ricoeur, might be extended trans-culturally in doing Asian Story Theology. Thanks to productive imagination, story theology might develop a creative hermeneutics with the stories of Asian culture and Biblical stories as its abundant resources and the Kingdom of God as its ultimate vision.

1. Story theology: Song's way of doing theology in Asia
Choan-Seng Song, a native Taiwanese, is regarded as one of the most famous and influential Asian Theologians. He dedicated himself to explore a new way of doing Theology in Asia. As Karl Federschmidt rightly observed, the theology of C. S. Song represented a new paradigm for doing *Theologieausasiatischen Quellen*.[2] In his book titled *God Who Risks Engagement: 12 Figures of Theologians and Philosophers of Religion in 20th Century*,[3] Henry Mottu put the name of C. S. Song, the only one from Asia, in the list of 12 prominent figures.

Song identifies himself consciously as an Asian theologian. Most of his works are related to Asia.[4] The main concern of Song is to find out a new way of doing theology in Asia and to distinguish it from Western traditional theology. Asia shall not be a theological colony, and Asian theologians shall define their own identities. Song coined several imaginative terms to describe his own theology: "theology of incarnation", "theology of transposition", "third-eye theology", "theology from womb of Asia", "theology of culture" and "story theology." If we want find out a spindle among them, it must be story theology.

In fact, Song was honored as a "guru of story theology."[5] In *Third Eye Theology*, he already used stories in Japanese Literature written by Miura Ayako (*Freezing Point*) and Endo Shusaku (*Silence*) to reorient the way of doing theology in Asia, but he did not yet use the term "story theology". In 1981, he was invited to give a keynote speech for "D.T. Niles Memorial Lecture" at the General Assembly Christian Conference of Asia (CCA). He tried to explore the meaning of political theology by interpreting a folk story. Later, this speech was expanded and published as a book titled *The Tears of Lady Meng—A Parable of People's Political Theology*. It was regarded as the masterpiece and a superb example of Song's story theology. Based on folk story told a thousand years ago yet still popular in Mandarin-speaking counties today, Song employed his theological imagination to interpret how the oppressed people resisted tyranny and dictatorship of the First Emperor of Chinese king for freedom, equality and justice—the heuristic visions of the Kingdom of God.

Story, in Song's understanding, is the very fountain of theology, because it contains the elements that give rise to theological thoughts such as metaphors, symbols and images.[6] For this reason, most of his important works were titled with story theology.[7] Song insisted that in doing theology it is stories rather than doctrines that matter primarily. In his trilogy of Asian Christology,[8] he intended to interpret the theological meaning of Jesus Christ in the contexts of Asian cultures. Stories of Jesus in the Four Gospels reveal how Jesus lived with the suffering people to seek for the Kingdom of God. The Kingdom of God provides the link between stories of Jesus and the stories of different cultures. He discerns the meaning of the Kingdom of God implied in the stories of Asian peoples in order to realize how God has lived among them and has revealed Himself to them. When the stories of Jesus Christ and stories of Asian people penetrate with each other, a theological space is opened for our theological imagination. With the stories of Jesus as the story of the Kingdom of God reflected in the stories of Asian cultures, we shall return to re-examine Christian theology with a new eye.

As we know, the Bible is full of stories and they are essential resources for doing theology. Song argues, however, that the stories of the Bible are not the only resources and shall not be used as exclusive in doing theology. There are abundant stories in the cultures outside of the Bible and Western Christianity, and they are important resources for doing theology. Asian theologians, who identify themselves as Asian, shall do theology with Asian cultural resources.[9]

2. Productive imagination in the reading of the Bible

Story is related to imagination, doing story theology means to do theology with imagination much more than with logical reasoning, though they do not contradict each other. Often, imagination is welcome for the performance of art, but is suspected as useless for knowing the truth. It is regarded as a faculty of free invention, a wandering thought without objective reference, a fiction deviated from true reality.

In contemporary philosophy, especially in hermeneutics, Ricoeur is the most noted philosopher who re-investigated the function of the imagination. According to his philosophical investigation, the denial of imagination originated from Plato. Imagination was exemplified by the model of copy and original: the image as copy is at best derivative from the original. While the original presents the reality, the copy and the image of it by imagination is a kind of re-presentation, a shadow, an illusion, a deception and even a distortion.[10] Ricoeur claimed, however, that imagination is related to myth, symbol, metaphor, narrative, and plays an inevitable role in the hermeneutical process of texts and reality. The most striking finding in his investigation is that imagination does not contradict reason; on the contrary, it permeates thought and conceptualization.[11] Imagination has *anoetic* function in seeking and re-describing reality. Productive imagination is not only positive but also necessary.

Ricoeur maintained that there are four domains of productive imagination[12]: (1) social & cultural imagination; (2) epistemological imagination; (3) poetic imagination[13] and (4) religious imagination. Within each domain there is power of imagination to portray an augmentation of reality whilst at the same time presenting a new way of looking at reality.[14] In "The Bible and the Imagination"[15] he investigates four presuppositions of the productive imagination of the fourth domain, especially in relation to the reading of the Bible.

(1) *Reading:* The act of reading itself is dynamic, it does not confine itself to repeating the meanings fixed in the text, but takes place as a prolonging of the itineraries of meaning opened up by the work of interpretation. From the perspective of hermeneutics, reading itself is "a key to the heuristic functioning of the productive imagination of texts."[16]

(2) *Narrative:* For Ricoeur, narrative is the mediation of our experience of time and the meaning of our existence."[T]ime becomes human time to the extent that it is organized after the manner of a narrative; narrative, in turn, is meaningful to the extent that it portrays the features of temporal experience."[17] This is why within the structure of the narrative we find an intersection between the text and life-experience that engenders imagination.[18] Narrative is a rule-governed invention and offers a remarkable example of the conjunction between fiction and re-description of the reality. In the Bible there is "indivisibly a narrative and a symbolic form of imagination."[19] The narrative of Exodus and the narrative of the Passion are the most decisive narrative kernels for all other narratives in the Old Testament and the New Testament and are inspiring for theological imagination.

(3) *Parable-Narrative:* The narrative-parable in the Bible, which is so distinguished in the teaching of Jesus on the Kingdom of God, is the key to an enigma[20] of the passage from a narrative to a paradigm and governs the passage from narrative to life. In this sense, narrative-parable is the best exemplar of a biblical form of embodied imagination."Parabolization is the metaphorization of a discourse. In the case of the narrative-parables, it consists of the metaphorization of a narrative taken as a whole."[21]

(4) *Intertextuality*: The intertextuality appears in the Bible as a key to the metaphorical transfer. Intertextuality consists of embedding one narrative in another narrative. It is the fundamental framework for the metaphorical transfer guided by the enigma-expression of the kingdom of God. There is a hermeneutic circle between the encompassing narrative and the embedded narrative.[22] Awareness of this hermeneutical circle will

avoid two errors of misinterpretation of narrative-parable: (1) to consider only the primary narrative and neglect its anchorage in another narrative and miss the function of metaphorization in the parable; (2) to reduce the parable to the speech-act of the personage whose story is recounted in the encompassing narrative without taking into account the transforming action exercised by the primary narrative on the encompassing narrative.[23]

Based on these four presuppositions, Ricoeur asserts that the very textual nature of the Bible reverberates a form of imagination within strategies of interpretation and thresholds of embodied meanings. By the function of imagination, the reading of the biblical text is a creative operation unceasingly employed in "decontextualizing its meaning and re-contextualizing it in today's *Sitz-im-Leben*."[24]

3. Productive imagination of story theology

It is interesting to note that these four presuppositions of productive imagination are implicitly demonstrated in the story theology of C. S. Song. In fact, Song's third-eye theology is kind of reading the Bible with Asian eyes shaped by Asian cultures. The meanings of the Bible are neither fixed nor determinate, it has its itineraries of meanings that are exposed to Asian eyes. While Ricoeur highlights narrative as the paradigm of imagination implied in the Bible, Song focuses on the stories as the loci for the theological imagination, and both of them regard the Kingdom of God as the enigma-expression of narrative (story). As to intertextuality, Song is more ambitious to extend it from the boundary within the Bible to a larger multi-cultural horizon.

There are two conspicuous points that display the productive imagination in the story theology of C. S. Song: (1) to read the Bible trans-culturally as well as inter-textually; (2) the metaphor of transposition as the quintessence of Incarnation.

In *Christian Mission in Reconstruction: An Asian Analysis*, Song made a shift from focusing on salvation history to the creation story. He found that the doctrine of salvation has narrowed down our vision of mission and theology, while a shift to the creation story would open our theological horizon. Song agrees that salvation and creation are inseparable; he claims, however, that when we start our theological thinking from the creation story rather than salvation history, we will be aware of a simple fact: since all nations and all peoples were created by God, there must be signs or traces of God's revelation in the histories and cultures of all nations and all peoples. These signs and traces are waiting for a mind with theological imagination to figure out their theological meanings.

Song's story theology asserts that we tell stories about God when we tell stories about Jesus Christ; and we tell the stories of Jesus Christ when we tell stories of the people with whom Jesus Christ lived.[25] Story theology does not use the stories of the Bible to exclude the stories of other cultures; on the contrary, it encourages dialogue and communication of stories between the stories of the Bible and the stories of Asian peoples.

The imaginative element of story theology is very obvious in Song's emphasis on the inevitability of the "transposition" of theology. In doing theology in the cultural contexts of non-Christian world, the truth of Kingdom of God has to be "trans-positional" rather than "propositional".

Transposition is a striking function of rendering similarity in the dissimilarity. Learning how to fit in a different culture is a matter of learning to discern "trans-modal" similarities between two dissimilar cultures. Theological wisdom is a matter of transposing biblical modes of speech and action into their contemporary counterparts of other cultures, in order to preserve the continuity and similarity between different cultural modals.

Song claimed that his theology was a "theology of transposition." He explored the "Exodus Model"[26] of salvation "transposing" it in different cultures. The story of Exodus was regarded as the model of theological thinking to interpret the meaning of salvation implied in the histories of Asian countries. Asian people suffered under the rule of colonial powers, fell in the sin of idolatry and looked forward to the hope of liberation. The subtitle of his famous book *The Compassionate God* is '*An Exercise in the Theology of Transposition.*' In it, Song maintained that transposition is a necessary approach to do theology in multi-religious and multi-cultural world as Asia. For the salvation of suffering peoples, the compassionate God had transposed Himself into different human cultures.

For Song, there are three dimensions of theological transposition.[27] (1) Transposition means the shift in space and time. The Christian gospel was transposed from Palestine to Greco-Roman world, afterword to the rest of the Europe and the West, and then to Asia and Africa. (2) Transposition means to translate the meanings of gospel of Jesus Christ written in Hebrew and Greek into other languages. The grammar, style, and manner of expression are different, but the essential meanings are dynamically equivalent. In this sense, transposition means also the communication of ideas, beliefs and meanings from one culture to another. (3) Transposition means Incarnation, God transposed Himself to the world and the Word became the flesh. In Incarnation, God risked becoming less than God and tasted the agony of God-forsakenness on the Cross. The Gospel of this incarnated God, when transposed from the biblical world to other cultural worlds, undergoes a change in itself as well as causes this world to change.

Concluding Remarks
The most striking feature of the Incarnation is trans-cultural. God's Word transposed into a particular culture context of human history, into a particular person of first-century Palestinian Jewish human being. Jesus identified with a particular cultural time and place, yet he transcended it. Jesus was in this world, yet he is not of the world. His life and work may thus be seen as a series of trans-cultural expressions of the kingdom of God. As God transposed his Word into humanity, so theology needs to transpose its languages, thought forms, and practices into diverse cultures. Doing theology is to continue the way of Jesus, imaging how he transposed himself into cultures. In this sense, transposition is an appropriate metaphor for productive imagination in doing theology. What story theology involves is not to "impose" supra-cultural truths and abstract principles, but to "transpose" the constant message of the Kingdom of God trans-culturally into the everyday life of the people.

To find out the similarity in dissimilar cultures, theologians must read the Bible with awareness of their own cultural conditionings. No theological statement is culture-free. In fact, the Bible itself is trans-cultural. The stories of the Bible propose something of trans-cultural significance and universal interest for our consideration. To affirm the story of the Bible as trans-cultural is not to say that it is "a-cultural" or "supra-cultural," rather it is to say that the Bible itself addresses to every culture.

Notes

1. This paper is based on the author's research project 'The Challenges and Opportunities of Digitalization for Taiwan's Contextual Theology' (109-2410-H-309-013-) with a grant from the Ministry of Science and Technology (MOST), Republic of China. Gratitude be to the MOST.
2. Karl H. Federschmidt, *Theologie aus asiatischen Quellen : der theologische Weg Choan-Seng Songs vor dem Hintergrund der asiatischen ökumenischen Diskussion* (Münster, Hamburg: LIT,1994).
3. *Dieu au risque de l'engagement: douze figures de la théologie et de la philosophie religieuse au XXe siècle; Suivi de La leçon d'adieu de l'auteur*, Henry Mottu (Genève: Labor et Fides, 2005). The other theologians in this list are: Karl Barth, Paul Tillich, Dietrich Bonhoeffer, Jürgen Moltmann, Hans Jonas, James Cone, Gustavo Gutiérrez, Leonardo Boff, Dorothée Sölle, Kä Mana and Martin Luther King. Mottu is a specialist in contemporary theologians and a professor of theology of Swiss University.
4. Such as *Christian Mission in Reconstruction—An Asian Attempt* (1975); 'Theology of Incarnation' in Gerald H. Anderson (ed.), *Asian Voices in Christian Theology* (1976); 'From Israel to Asia: A Theological Leap' (1976); *Third-Eye Theology: Theology in Formation in Asian Settings* (1981); 'God's Politics of Construction', in England J. C. (ed.), *Living Theology in Asia* (1981, pp.72-76); *Tell Us Our Names: Story Theology from an Asian Perspective* (1984); *Theology from the Womb of Asia* (1986); 'Freedom of Christian Theology for Asian Cultures: Celebrating the Inauguration of the Programme for Theology and Cultures in Asia' (1989); and his famous trilogy *The Cross in the Lotus World: Jesus, the Crucified People* (1990); *Jesus and the Reign of God* (1993); *Jesus in the Power of the Spirit* (1994).
5. John C. England, Jose Kuttianmattathilsdb, John Mansford Prior svd. Luly A. Quintons rd. David Suh Kwang-sun & Janice Wickeri, (eds.) *Asian Christian Theologies, A Research Guide to Authors, Movements, Sources.* Vol. 3 (Northeast Asia. ISPCK/Claretian Publishers/ Orbis Books:2004), 688-691.
6. Choan-Seng Song, *In the Beginning Were Stories, Not Texts: Story Theology*, (Eugene, Oregon: Cascade Books, 2011), 18.
7. For example, *Tell Us Our Names: Story Theology from an Asian Perspective* (1984); *The Believing Heart—An Invitation to Story Theology* (1999), *In the Beginning Were Stories, Not Texts—Story Theology* (2010).
8. They are: *Jesus, the Crucified People* (1989), *Jesus and the Reign of God* (1993), *Jesus in the Power of the Spirit* (1994).
9. This guiding line of doing theology is implemented by Programme for Theology and Cultures in Asia (PTCA) founded on 1984. Choan-Seng Song was the first director of PTCA.
10. George H. Taylor, 'Ricoeur's Philosophy of Imagination', *Journal of French Philosophy* 16, no. 1/2 (2006): 93-104.
11. Taylor, 'Ricoeur's Philosophy of Imagination', 94.
12. Ricoeur claimed himself as a hearer of the Word, a philosopher who dialogued with theologians and biblical exegetes. He explains his positon in the Preface of André LaCoque and Paul Ricoeur, *Thinking Biblically. Exegetical and Hermeneutic Studies*, trans. by David Pellauer (Chicago: University of Chicago Press, 1998) ix-xix. Ricoeur's philosophy and hermeneutics had influenced contemporary theology.
13. For Ricoeur, the poetic texts have the ability to disclose a view of a possible world that, in the process of reading, eclipses the tangible, objective world. William David Hall, 'The Economy of Gift: Paul Ricoeur's Poetic Re-description of Reality', *Literature & Theology*, 20/2 (2006):189–204, 193.
14. Taylor, 'Ricoeur's Philosophy of Imagination', 97-100.
15. Paul Ricoeur, 'The Bible and the Imagination', in *Figuring the Sacred: Religion, Narrative, and Imagination*, trans. David Pellauer, ed. Mark I. Wallace (Minneapolis: Fortress Press, 1995):144-166.
16. Ricoeur, 'The Bible and the Imagination', 145-146.

17. Paul Ricoeur, *Time and Narrative*, Vol 1, trans. by K. McLaughlin and D. Pellauer (Chicago-London: University of Chicago Press, 1984), 3. On Page 52, Ricoeur expressed in another way, "Time becomes human to the extent that it is articulated through a narrative mode, and narrative attains its full meaning when it becomes a condition of temporal existence."
18. Ricoeur, *Time and Narrative*, Vol 1, 52-53. Ricoeur maintained a theory of threefold of mimesis, to demonstrate how mimesis (productive imagination) plays in the intersection of narrative-text and lived experience.
19. Ricoeur, 'The Bible and the Imagination', 145. Ricoeur restricted myself in this article on the category of narrative texts, although he knew that there are other categories such as poem, wisdom, proverb, ritual...etc.
20. Ricoeur appropriated the term "enigma" of Ivan Almeida to interpret the meaning of revelation. As Richard Niebuhr claimed in *Meaning of Revelation*, the revelation means the intelligible event of Jesus Christ as the righteousness, power and wisdom of God makes all other events intelligible.
21. Ricoeur, 'The Bible and the Imagination', 161.
22. Ricoeur said that the "Narrative-Parable of the Wicked Husbandmen" (Mark 12:1-12; Matt l 21:33-46; Luke 20:9-19) was embedded in encompassing narrative of Isaiah 1:1-11: "My beloved had a vine-yard [...] For the vineyard of the Lord of Hosts is the house of Israel." In fact, "vineyard" is a metaphor appears often in the Bible.
23. Ricoeur, 'The Bible and the Imagination', 150.
24. Ricoeur, 'The Bible and the Imagination', 145.
25. Choan-Seng Song, *Jesus the Crucified People: The Cross in the Lotus World*, Volume I (Minneapolis: Fortress Press, 1996), 37.
26. Choan-Seng Song, 'New China and Salvation History: A Methodological Enquiry', *South East Asia Journal of Theology*, 15/2 (1974):52-67.
27. Choan-Seng, Song, *The Compassionate God: An Exercise in the Theology of Transposition* (London: SCM. 982), 5-12.

Asian Liberation Theologies in Times of Populism

DANIEL F. PILARIO

This article attempts to recover the liberationist current in Asian theologies and reflect on the challenges presented to it by our dominant populist contexts. It discusses the liberation themes in Asian theologies in general; the context of Philippine liberation theologies, in particular; the challenges posed by populist movements and discourses; and, lastly, attempts to articulate some directions for liberation theologies in the times of populism.

A stereotypic mapping of theological developments outside Europe and the United States after Vatican II runs thus: liberation theologies emerged out of Latin America; inculturation out of Africa and interreligious dialogue out of Asia. These general developments caught the attention of Vatican authorities and their concerns also traveled continentally. In 1996, Joseph Ratzinger—then the Prefect of the CDF and later Pope Benedict XVI—wrote: "In the '80s, the theology of liberation in its radical forms seemed to be the most urgent challenge for the faith of the church...[After the demise of Marxism] relativism has thus become the central problem for the faith of the present time."[1] From issuing directives against Latin American liberation theologies (1986), he turned his gaze to the plural theologies of religions, characteristic of Asian Christianity, (1990s) ending in the magisterial position of *Ecclesia in Asia* (1999). This article intends to go beyond these stereotypes; it attempts to recover the liberationist themes in Asian theologies, and reflect on its challenges in the present populist context. It has four parts: a discussion on the liberationist themes in Asian Theologies in general; liberation theologies in the Philippines, in particular; the challenges posed by populist movements and discourses; and an attempt to articulate some directions for liberation theologies in the times of populism.

Liberationist Thematic in Asian Theologies

A good number of Asian theologians have clearly articulated the active presence of liberationist themes in Asian theologies.[2] Though similar in inspiration and values, Christian liberation theologies are not mere copycats or ideological transfers of their Latin American counterparts. They are responses to actual situations and cultures in the Asian continent. The *Dalit* theology of India is a response to the marginalization of the untouchable caste who find themselves in the lowest cultural and socio-economic ladder of the Indian society. Religious conversion of Dalits into Christianity or Buddhism does not erase the entrenched habitus and structures of centuries-old casteism. A theology working towards their liberation rethinks Christian categories, for instance, of God becoming *Dalit* in Jesus, the suffering servant who led them towards freedom.[3]

In Korea, *minjung* theology emerged from protests of the labor movement in the context of Korean industrialization in the 1950s to the 1970s. *Minjung* (literally the "mass of people") refers to "those who are oppressed politically, exploited economically, alienated socially, and kept uneducated in cultural and intellectual matters".[4] Rereading biblical themes into the Korean history, which was tainted by colonial foreign domination, or translating the bible into local languages of the peoples, or empowering women who are central figures of Korean family, became the preoccupation of Protestant theologians who pioneered *minjung* theology.

Less known is *burakumin* theology in Japan, whose name is derived from the untouchable group ("hamlet people") of outcasts of the feudal Japanese social hierarchy. Though officially abolished in 1868, their descendants numbering to around three million today continue to suffer stigma and discrimination. Since the 1920s, the *burakumin* liberation movement—though not Christian—was inspired the metaphor of the "crown of thorns" and later on taken on by theologians concerned with their liberation.[5] Other theological developments in Asia also exhibit decolonial and liberationist currents—"waterbuffalo theology" (Thailand), the "pain of God" theology (Japan), "third eye theology" or "*yin yang* theology" (China, Taiwan and Korea), planetary theology (Sri Lanka), ecological and feminist theologies (Ecclesia of Women in Asia), among others.

A cursory look at ancient Asian religions displays the liberationist theme as inherent to their own traditions. According to Michael Amaladoss,[6] the ultimate purpose of Hindu religious practice is liberation *(moksha)* which can interpreted both as cosmic liberation or creation of a just society here and now governed by *dharma* as underlying order of reality. Indian social reformers like Swami Vivekanda (1863-1902) and Mahatma Gandhi (1869-1948) have emphasized the social activist part of Hindu tradition. In their thinking, *karma* is not seen as blaming the victims for one's state of life as empowering them with possibilities to change their circumstances.[7] If there is an indwelling divinity in all beings, the human-divine bifurcation is denied, thus, to serve others also means to serve the divine. Following Vivekanda, Gandhi writes: "The service of the distressed, the crippled, the helpless among living things constitutes worship to God."[8] For its part, Buddhism has been traditionally seen as a world-denying religion seeking freedom in *nirvana* (emptiness) personified is the monk's absolute detachment. But Amaladoss points to social reformers like Bhikku Buddhadasa (1906-1993) of Thailand or Thich Nhat Hanh of Vietnam to show the possibilities of a socially engaged Buddhism.

For these authors, *nirvana* is not emptiness of being but emptiness of the ego towards a life of interdependence with other beings. "One need not quit the world in pursuit of *nirvana*. One must rather be and act in the world... to have concern for the whole, to live with restraint and generosity and to treat others with respect and kindness."[9] The same is true with Confucianism. Its concern with harmony with nature also means harmony with the community which can engender the social virtues of courtesy, generosity, good faith, kindness and peace. Islam—a victim of its violent stereotype—actually aims for the liberation of the oppressed and restoration of the dignity of the Muslim people. Islamic monotheism in fact symbolizes its own aspirations for unity, justice and equality. To conclude, the liberationist themes emerging out of these ancient religions—e.g., inclusive liberation, non-dualist existence, harmony with people and nature, political kindness and tenderness—simultaneously complements, critiques and expands the religious worldviews of our Christian liberation theologies.

Liberationist Theologizing in the Philippines: Beyond the Theology of Struggle

On surface, the "theology of struggle"—as the liberation theology in the Philippines was called—is considered a direct descendant of its Latin American counterpart. Beyond this assessment, however, it might be good to provide a wider historical and cultural context to the liberationist theologizing in the Philippines.[10] Somewhere, I attempted to map contemporary contextual theologies in the Philippines. First, there are mainstream theologies that start off with the positions of the Magisterium and attempt to extrapolate their relevance into contemporary times. These theologies do not merely parrot the teachings of the Popes and encyclicals. They are contextual applications of the magisterial themes as they are needed on the ground by pastors, missionaries, religious and lay leaders in the heart of the pastoral field. These seemingly centrist theological directionsare not conservative at all. They provide answers to the actual questions of the poor; they are timely creative reflections, making sense of real struggles that people undergo in daily life. They are echoes of "everyday liberation" articulated in the language of the people,viewed through the lens of the gospel and sound Church teaching, expressed in songs, stories and popular religious practices learned from childhood in the context of community celebrations.

The second trend is a response to the challenge of inculturation. Many of these theologians start with cultural analysis as the ground of their theological reflection. Aspects of the cultures—either from the lowland or indigenous population—are woven into theological themes and correlated with the Christian tradition. Recovery of cultural worldviews buried by centuries of colonization and the decisive use of local resources shape the structure of contextual theologies as it critiques dominant Western theologies in the local scene and their use of foreign philosophical categories. Even before post-liberationist theological currents gained currency, the Philippine inculturationist direction appears to be the forerunner of the now famous decolonial and postcolonial theologies.

The third trend—famous in the 1980s during the Marcos dictatorship—is the classic liberation theology dubbed by international theologians as "theology of struggle"[11] occasioned by the repression of the Martial Law of Marcos. Some of these theologians belong to the communist resistance movement; others do not have ideological affiliation but ground their theologies in the prophetic challenge of the gospel. In the context of the cruel repression of the 1970s where people were just killed or made to disappear, these two directions were not substantially different. They were fighting one single enemy: the dictatorial regime of Marcos.

However, I would like to expand the reflection on this liberationist thematic in the contextual theologies in the Philippines. Though the theologies of the Spanish regime in the Philippines was mainly in collusion with colonial power, there were cracks in the iron curtain that gave way to resistance theologies even under colonial rule. Contemporary authors like Reynaldo Iletopoint to the oblique resistance practiced by revolutionaries by employing religious rituals like the Pasyon (which ends in the resurrection) to envision a new world of freedom and equality outside the colonizers' gaze.[12] In fact, the local population welcomed the Spanish priests into the locality to fight against the abuses of the soldiers. There is a long history of liberationist reflection in the Philippines even among the first missionaries who came with the colonizers. Among them was Domingo de Salazar, the first bishop of Manila, a faithful student of Francisco Vitoria of the famous School of Salamanca of the colonial period who, together with Bartolome de las Cases in Latin America, defended the rights of the indigenous people against the Iberian colonization project. After a long fight with colonial rulers in the Philippines, Salazar went back to Spain in 1591 to put his lifetime advocacy in front of the King. "It is clear then that the dominion over those Islands could not have come to belong to the King our lord either by title of election or of just war," he argues.[13] These colonial missionaries defended the rights of the Filipinos against Spanish sovereignty, particularly against slavery and extortion of tribute. In the later stage of Spanish colonization, people experienced the cruelty of the colonialists and the friars. In response, an educated Christian class, after having studied abroad, launched the revolutionary uprising against Spain. Also, the history of our revolutionary Filipino clergy is a well-documented phenomenon of Philippine history.[14] Motivated by the biblical vision of liberation and the Christian rhetoric of freedom, the disgruntled masses and their leaders revolted and overthrew their Spanish colonial masters. My point is simple: from the encounter of Christianity and the Philippine cultures 500 years ago, liberation and resistance theologies can already be discerned. This is an assertion that we need to consider in these times when majority of Christians—bishops, priests and religious included—are allergic to liberation theology.

Populism and its Challenge to Liberationist Religions
One of the present challenges to liberation theologies is populist thinking. Populism as a political force is not new. But recent events with Trump, Bolsonaro or Erdogan, for example, made it infamous worldwide. Growing populist governments are surprisingly gaining massive popular support. They exhibit necessary rhetorical but also physical violence needed both to keep people in place. Ironically, populism identifies politics with two homogenous and imagined bodies of population—"the people" who are adjudged to be good and "the elite" who are condemned to be evil. This good-evil spectrum is a common practice of populist religious thinkers as they "resort to the 'Manic heist' worldview in reference to the ancient religious movement whose radical worldview divided the world into the diametrically conflicting principles of Light and Darkness to describe the centrality of such dualism in the populist worldview."[15] In this moral framing, populism exhibits its intrinsic relationship with religions. Religious populism is two-dimensional: one is overtly religious, the "politization of religion". This "manifestation of religious populism proclaims to be following, or fulfilling, the will and plans of the Almighty—with whom the groups feel, and believe, that they have a privileged relationship".[16] It looks at itself as fighting Godless enemies in the name of God. The religious language of the "Make America Great Again" (MAGA) movement is a good example. Trump was seen as the "white Jesus" and his rallies were reminiscent of the "big tent religious revivals" in the 18th century American Pentecostalism.[17] The second dimension is the "sacralization of politics" which aims to pervade modern politics with the language of the sacred in order to set a group as an "absolute transcendent force that will fundamentally change mundane everyday evil politics".[18] A good number of conservative faith affiliations coming from evangelical and mainline churches which anoint rightist political leaders can be cited as example. These two dimensions look distinct but they actually overlap on the ground. These seemingly

unbreakable relationship between religions and populist politics already makes it difficult for liberation theology to prosper.

Let me contextualize these directions in the Philippine milieu. For the past five years (since 2016), the Philippines finds itself in the international headlines as sharing in a distinctly populist climate. The present government led by our President Rodrigo Duterte exhibits the identical characteristics of all other populist leaders worldwide. He displays paternalistic governance in all places. "We" (the poor ordinary people) vs. "them" (the elite and oligarchs) characterizes his policies. Those who do not fit his schemes are "othered"; many of them are silenced, others sidelined and eliminated. This is not mere rhetoric but violent action. For instance, according to some estimates, his police and their associates have killed 33,000+ drug addicts because they do not fit his banner program of a drug-free Philippines. He has also killed human rights activists, indigenous peoples, their lawyers, and others. This continues even in the midst of the pandemic.

What interests me is the religious scene. What is the theological response to this populist governance in the Philippines? One can identify a range of responses—from liberationist resistance to religious support of the regime. Let me focus on a substantial group of the Christian right who lend theological justification to the Duterte regime. A good number of the population belong to the so-called megachurches whose theology provides the characteristically populist response—an intersection between the sacralization of politics and politization of religion. The Filipino sociologists, Jayeel Cornelio and Ia Maranon, identify the common characteristics of the theology of these megachurches.[19] First is its notion of divine authority which props up violent regimes. Many of these churches read Romans 13:1 literally: "Let every person be subject to the governing authorities; for there is no authority except from God, and those authorities that exist have been instituted by God." For them, Duterte is truly God-sent. He is the anointed leader to heal this nation because our situation needs such divine intervention. A research done in Payatas, where I work on weekends, has one pastor arguing on Duterte's War on Drugs: "Duterte as president is clearly an act of God to 'teach the country a lesson'. He believes that drug addiction is a sinful condition that has its own consequences. The violence of the War on Drugs is at one level a divine judgment and he leaves it up to the government to fully execute it. At another, the anti-drug campaign is meant to convince the rest of the public of what sin does in the end."[20]

Second is this theology's apolitical dimension. Many of these churches fosters apolitical theologies. Since the world is ambivalent, Christians better not engage the world — almost literally applying "we are in the world but not of the world" discourse in the gospel of John (17:16). If there is prophetism, it is not found in political engagement; it is in serving as "contrast communities", living a totally different life than the rest of the world around. However, in the experience of the Philippines, many of these Churches anoint Christian leaders, pray over them, endorse them in elections all in exchange of political favors. This dualistic theological frame makes their members all supporters of Duterte's regime.

The third characteristic is the belief in prosperity theology among the middle class members. The class demographics already hint at its politically conservative position. If business is good, why rock the boat? This theology also looks to the bible for support, for instance, Deuteronomy 8:18: "Remember the Lord your God, for it is he who gives you power to get wealth, so that he may confirm his covenant that he swore to your ancestors." Prosperity theologians assert having the right belief, right thinking and right doing to achieve wealth.[21] And since Duterte campaigned to create economic prosperity in the Philippines, these Christians are automatically Duterte supporters, even if the pandemic has sent the Philippines way down in the economic ladder.

To sum up: first, all these characteristics are present in the megachurches across denominational divide—evangelical, Protestants and Catholics alike. Second, all theological arguments converge to preserve the status quo, and are thus supportive of the present populist government. Third, the majority Christian population who are seemingly neutral and non-engaged in fact find this dualistic, privatized theology convenient for political non-involvement regardless of this government's corruption and incompetence, killing and violence, violation of human rights and blatant disregard of human dignity.

Articulating Directions for Liberation Theologies
This brings me to my last point: the uphill climb of prophetic resistance

and liberation theologies in the context of populist regimes. The waning of liberation theologies worldwide is not a new phenomenon. It has been experienced in Latin America and elsewhere caused by many factors. Philosophically, we know of the collapse of metanarratives in postmodernity; there has also been the turn to culture discourse in the social sciences that rejects the hard Marxist economic analysis reminiscent of the first periods of liberation theologies. Theologically, we have also experienced the anti-liberationist stance of the long pontificates of John Paul II and Benedict XVI. The "ad intra" concerns for doctrine, liturgy and church discipline during these times have eclipsed the need of engagement with the world and the poor characteristic of Vatican II — something that Pope Francis only starts to recover. All these present cultural phenomena of populism have eclipsed liberation theologies in the churches and academy. In the end, let me outline some of the challenges to liberation theology in particular, and to the Church, in general.

First, there is a need to reassert prophetic theologizing. In the context of blatant disregard of human dignity coupled with the real poverty among our people, there is a need to recover prophetic theologies in our times. The forms can vary, and they should, but the prophets need to stand up to the kings as it was in the Old Testament. Yet beyond the Jewish-Christian discourse, there is a need to revisit the prophetic intuitions of Asian religions we have narrated in the beginning. These Asian religious resources engrained in the habitus of Asian peoples can be tapped to inspire resistance and work for justice. As Catholic Christians, we also have along tradition of the Social Teaching of the Church which outlines the contents and positions on social issues consistent with the gospel. How to bring this "well-kept" secret to our grassroots communities should be a service theologians and pastoral workers should creatively strive for, especially in these times when these same communities are under attack by the apologists of populist politics.

The second challenge is to restructure theological reflection and formation at all levels from the top down to grassroots communities. If theologies prop up populist regimes, theologies should also ground resistance. A restructuring of the theological curriculum in seminaries and the access of lay people to theological formation are necessary towards making liberation theologies speak again. We need to ask what kind of theologies are taught in our seminaries and theological centers. Beyond these traditional centers of learning, however, we need to ask how accessible is liberationist theological formation to grassroots communities. Resistance does not start with synods, or with theologians and church authorities. Theologies of liberation can only start from the lives of the victims, from the ground of suffering itself. Like the initial stirrings of liberation in Asia—*Dalits, minjung, burakumin*—the victims are the real prophets of our times. Their lives are themselves lives of resistance.

The third challenge is to theologically recover the liberationist character of everyday life. Populist discourses thrive on people's discontent with daily life and everyday suffering brought about by harsh global economy, political authoritarianism and climate change. Religions and their theologies that do not respond to these longings for liberation and well-being risk becoming irrelevant. The demise of theological metanarratives—be it metaphysical or liberational—no longer attract people. Our grassroots communities do not have access to arduous argumentation and voluminous *summas*. Their urgent questions demand urgent answers. The Filipino theologian, Catalino Arevalo, talks about theologizing in "bits and pieces", a theology on the spot, done in an *ad hoc* manner, a theology *in via*, of a people also on its way. It is a theology done together "in hours of doing and suffering, in emptiness, in confusion and paralysis, in struggle, sometimes in anguish and despair, sometimes with the shedding of real blood and tears."[22] Liberation theologies—done with the people, among the people, in their language and idioms, in their place and time, in response to their suffering and aspiration—proves to be a necessary form of the prophetic theology of everyday resistance.

Notes

+ Gratitude to the Vincentian Center for Church and Society, St. John's University, New York, for the time and space to write this article.
1. Joseph Cardinal Ratzinger, 'Relativism: The Central Problem of Faith Today', in https://www.ewtn.com/catholicism/library/relativism-the-central-problem-for-faith-today-2470 (accessed 07.06.2021).
2. Cf. Aloysius Pieris, *Asian Theology of Liberation* (London: T & T Clark, 1988); Michael Amaladoss, *Life in Freedom: Liberation Theologies from Asia* (Maryknoll, NY: Orbis, 1997); Felix Wilfred, ed., *Leave the Temple: Indian Paths to Human Liberation* (Maryknoll, NY: Orbis, 1992); Peter Phan, 'Experience and Theology: An Asian Liberation Perspective', *ZeitschriftfürMissionswissenschaft und Religionswissenschaft* 77 (1993): 99-121.
3. Sathianathan Clarke, *Dalits and Christianity: Subaltern Religion and Liberation Theology in India*

(Oxford: Oxford University Press, 200).
4. Cyris Moon and Hŭi-sŏk Mun, *A Korean Minjung Theology: An Old Testament Perspective* (Maryknoll, NY: Orbis, 1985), 1.
5. TeruoKuribayashi, 'A Theology of the Crown of Thorns: Towards the Liberation of Asian Outcasts', Ph.D. Dissertation, Union Theological Seminary, 1987; Kuribayashi, 'Recovering Jesus for Outcasts in Japan', https://nirc.nanzan-u.ac.jp/nfile/4133 (accessed 09.09.2021).
6. Michael Amaladoss, 'Liberation Theologies from Asia', *Laval théologique et philosophique* 54, No. 3 (October 1998): 529-541.
7. Cf. Stephen Long, '"Work Is Worship" Swami Vivekananda's Philosophy of Seva and its Contribution to the Gandhian Ethos', *Post-Christian Interreligious Liberation Theology*, eds. H. S. Timani and L. S. Ashton (London: Palgrave Macmillan, 2021), 81-98; Marc Pugliesi, 'Looking Upon All Beings as One's Self: Insights from Advaita Hinduism for Racial Justice Within Christian Theology and Liberative Praxis', *Post-Christian Interreligious Liberation Theology*, 99-125.
8. Ignatius Jesudasan, *A Gandhian Theology of Liberation* (Maryknoll, NY: Orbis Books, 1984), 70.
9. Michael Amaladoss, 'Liberation Theologies from Asia', 536.
10. D. F. Pilario, 'The Craft of Contextual Theology: Towards a Methodological Conversation in the Philippine Context', *Hapag: An Interdisciplinary Theological Journal*, 1(2004), Issue No. 1: 5-39.
11. Eleazar Fernandez, *Toward a Theology of Struggle* (Eugene, OR: Wipf and Stock, 1994).
12. Reynaldo Ileto, *Pasyon and Revolution: Popular Movements in the Philippines 1840-1910* (Quezon City: Ateneo de Manila University Press, 1979).
13. Cf. John Schumacher, 'Bishop Domingo de Salazar and the Manila Synod of 1582', in *Growth and Decline: Essays in Philippine Church History* (Quezon City: Ateneo de Manila University Press, 2009), 1-21.
14. John Schumacher, *Revolutionary Clergy: The Filipino Clergy and the Nationalist Movement 1850-1903* (Manila: Ateneo de Manila University Press, 1981).
15. José Pedro Zúquete, 'Populism and Religion' in *Oxford Handbook of Populism*, eds. Cristobal Rovira Katwasser et al. (Oxford: Oxford University Press, 2017), 445.
16. *Ibid.*
17. S. Romi Mukherjee, 'Make America Great Again as White Political Theology', *Revue LISA* 15, No. 2 (2018), https://journals.openedition.org/lisa/9887
18. José Pedro Zúquete, 'Populism and Religion' in *Oxford Handbook of Populism*, eds. Cristobal Rovira Katwasser et al., 446.
19. Jayeel Cornelio and Ia Maranon, '"A 'Righteous Intervention'": Megachurch Christianity and Duterte's War on Drugs in the Philippines', *International Journal of Asian Christianity* 2 (2019): 211-230.
20. Jayeel Cornelio and Erron Medina, 'Christianity and Duterte's War on Drugs in the Philippines', *Politics, Religion & Ideology* 20:2 (2019): 151-169.
21. Erron Medina and Jayeel Cornelio, 'Neoliberal Christianity and the Rise of the New Prosperity Gospel in the Philippines', *Pneuma* 43 (2021) 72-93.
22. C. Arevalo, 'After Vatican II: Theological Reflection on the Church in the Philippines 1965-1987', *Landas* 2 (1988): 17.

Vietnamese Theology in the Making

TRAN VAN DOAN

Responding to the Second Vatican Council's call for promoting culture in its relation to Christian faith (Gaudium et Spes, 53-62), Asian theologies emerge as a part of 'aggiornamento'. Unfortunately, they are condemned as unfit by the Sacred Congregation of the Doctrine of the Faith (CDF). Against such verdict, this paper argues that the problem is the CDF's inadequate understanding of the Asian way of living with God. I contend that beneath the difference about God between Christianity and Asian cultures there is a common understanding of God in terms of life and of union as a way of being in God. I take the Chinese and Vietnamese cultures as an example to show that their understanding of God in terms of life, and union as a way to live in God can be of help to overcome the seemingly unbridgeable difference. The paper consists of two main parts: the first part studies the difference between Christianity and Chinese/Vietnamese cultures from the perspective of logical thinking: CDF's theologians think in terms of logo-centrism while Chinese and Vietnamese theologians in terms of the way of living. The second part is a sketch of the logic of heart with its the main principles and characteristics that Vietnamese theologians take for theology: maternity, reasonableness, union as a way of life, pluralism and openness.

1. Introductory Remarks

Asian theology, a subject once frozen by the Sacred Congregation for the Doctrine of the Faith (CDF), again captivates the attention of theologians amid the global crisis of Christianity. Actually, the hasty accusation that Asian theologians are voicing their heretical tones supporting pluralism, breaking the harmonious communion and hurting the unity of the Holy

Church, is still there. As of now, this "offense" is not outright condemned but rather carefully monitored because the CDF knew too well that any confrontation with Asian theologians may reopen the old wounds of the "rites conflict" in the 17th-18th centuries — an unfortunate episode that has hurt Christians for centuries.[1]

But what offense? Heresy or separatism? That is not the case. Asian theologians' faith in God and loyalty to the Church are beyond any doubt (as seen in the cases of Tisa Balasuriya, Jacques Dupuis, Aloysius Pieris, Peter C. Phan and others). In my view, the real issue here is the CDF's refusal to recognize the Asian way of living *with* God as a legitimate way without a thorough knowledge of it, and its dogmatic imposition of its own Roman-centric logic on Asian theology without a serious reflection on the inner relation between living and thinking. The claim of the Roman-centric thinking as the unique way of and to the truth would logically exclude anyway of thinking unfit to its form and its contents.

The Roman-centric speculative view is contested, however. It contradicts the fact that it is the way of living that is shaping human thinking; it bypasses the Church's teachings that God reveals, expresses, communicates and acts in different ways, languages, and cultures. Based on Neo-Platonism and Aristotelianism, themselves the products of the Hellenistic life-world, a Roman-centric mode of thinking can no longer be adequate to represent the global-world, a world of diverse cultures, religions, philosophies, arts, etc. Hence, the emergence of Asian theologies should be seen not as a sign of schism but rather as an "aggiornamento" i.e. an effort to enrich theology, making the Church more universal and ecumenical and its teachings more practicable and receptive to non-Christian Asia.

This paper is an attempt to understand theology from the perspective of the Chinese and Vietnamese way of living. I argue that the wide gap between Vietnamese culture and Christianity could be reduced to a significant degree if theology is constructed from the way of living that is guided by the principle of harmonious union. I begin with a short presentation of the difference between the Roman-centric thinking *of* God and the Asian way of living *with* God and continue with an analysis of their interpretation of the principle of unity: unity as unification for Roman-centric thinkers and unity as union for Vietnamese theologians. Vietnamese theology, presented as an example of how the Viet way of living *with* God, can contribute to Christian theology, making it more appealing to non-Christians in Vietnam.

2. The Difference
The rites-controversy seemed to head towards a "happy end" with Pius XII's decree *Plane compertum* (1939) after over two centuries of deadlock since Clement XI's *Cum Deus optimus* (1704). Part of the once forbidden rites is regarded as socio-cultural, and hence "permitted". Actually, that is far from an end. The word "permission" itself implies special treatment for a particular case that can be easily revoked.[2] Permission is determined not by the rightness or legitimacy of Chinese rites but rather by Rome's toleration. Basically, the difference between Catholic Church and Confucians on matters of magisterium and traditions remains with no real reconciliation in sight.

This "incommensurability" can be seen in the conflicting views on God and human relation to God.[3] Unlike Christianity which takes God as the center, Chinese culture is concerned rather with the questions of how to generate, maintain and foster life. Unlike sacraments and liturgy as human devotional acts to God, Chinese rites express human gratitude and moral obligation to benefactors (the Heaven, the Earth, ancestors, parents, heroes, teachers) and great personalities. The Chinese are not obsessed with the question of who is God but rather with how God impacts on their life. Confucius' apparent lack of interests for the metaphysical question about God and spiritual beings (Analects 6:20) and his concern over humanity (Analects 10:11) do not contradict his belief and trust in God (Analects 3:12; 8:19) and in the spiritual world (Analects 3:12). His humanism is theistic in the sense that human life cannot be possible without the participation of the Heaven (*tian*/天) and the Earth (*di*/地), and in form of union (天人合一) (The Book of Changes.) In short, the Chinese mind is obsessed more with actual life (*sheng*/生) and happy life,[4] and less with God or the life after death. In the eyes of Roman-centric theologians, Confucius' focus on life apparently opposes the Christian belief in God as the only One, omnipotent and absolute; in the original sin and the role of Christ as redeemer; and in a transcendent world.[5]

A great number of Chinese theologians are well aware of the above enigmas. Their efforts at building a Chinese theology with its own categories aim at finding a commonality that can be accepted by the CDF and conservative Confucians.[6] For such aim, they wisely avoid to deal openly with the unreasonable imposition of the Roman-centric thinking on them.

I agree with my Chinese colleagues in principle. However, I see in the imposition of any kind of logo-centrism a serious threat to the intercultural dialogue promoted by the Church. Roman-centric theologians are accustomed to view the world according to the image speculated by themselves, and consequently, demand the world of theologians to be fit to their model. They overlook the fact that it is the living world which is the source of thinking, and not the reverse. Difference, pluralism, conflicts are factually a part of the living world that cannot be dismissed by a simple formal logic.

Asian sages know this truth when they start with the living and not the thinking, with action and not reasoning. Buddha begun his mission with an awareness of the actually suffering world, while Confucius started with his search for practical solutions to social disorder, endless wars and injustice.

3. Identity as Belongingness and Unity as Union – Attempt to Go Beyond Differences

This section aims at showing that the principle of identity and the demand for unity could be understood in terms of (Chinese) harmonious union instead of (Roman-centric) unification. To facilitate the discussion, I will present the logic of Roman-centric thinking and the Chinese/Vietnamese way of living as condensed as possible.

Roman-centric thinkers opt for speculative and formal logic, with fixed aims and calculative means. It obeys the principle of identity and non-contradiction, the one seen in the Aristotelian syllogism. God, the Creator and the One, is taken as the undisputed major premise while all creatures from God as the minor premise. Accordingly, the truth in the conclusion must be the same God, the One and the All, the Beginning and the End (Exodus 3:14). God is the Unifier (Ephesians 2:11-12) because unity is His substance, and unification His means. Disunity, or lack of unity, mean revolt, heresy, chaos (Gen 11:1-9) or schism.

Chinese theologians adopt different logics with focus on life as premise, and practical consequences as conclusion. Since life is the sign of God's presence, all ways of life are occurring harmoniously in accordance with His plan. And since union (合/hợp) is the way of life as seen in the coupling of different elements(*yin* and *yang*, female and male, human and nature, etc.), union is preferred over unification (同一).

Union happens in two ways: the inner way and the outer way. The inner way (*tâm đạo*/心道) is the way of union with God and spiritual beings, while the outer way is a union with nature (自然) and human fellows (人道).[7] Both inner and outer life are guided by the innate desire for happiness that can be realized by an ideal union with God and nature (天時地利人和), and among humans. Those who cultivate and fulfill humanity are praised as the just, the noble (君子), the wise (聖賢), the heroic (英雄) and venerated as saints (聖人).

As I see, the Chinese conception of union is close to the one emphasized by Christ in words and deeds. He is identified with the God Father in the sense of being in union with his Father. And so is his identification with the Church which is itself a union of all Christians. Christian identity is defined by the act of participating in the union and not by the abandonment of one's own root, traditions and language (The Acts 2:6-12). Identity here is understood in terms of belongingness[8] instead of "sameness"; and union as a deliberate participation without renouncing particularity as a part of one's own identity.

4, The Logic of the Heart as the Viet Way
The Viet(越) are forced by the Han (漢) invaders to take Han's script as the official means of communication, and Confucianism as state ideology during a thousand-year-occupation. Despite their remarkable success to resist China's "sinicization"(漢化) and maintain total independence since 938 AD, they are still deeply influenced by Han cultures. That explains a great similarity but also a certain difference between the Chinese way and the Vietnamese way. Actually, the Viet distinguish themselves from the Han in many aspects, havingtheir own way of living and thinking.[9] Basically, the Vietnamese way of living can be understood from the principle "of life" and "for life", which is concretely seen in the Viet's view on maternity, the reasonable, the logic of heart, union and pluralism. As consequence, God and humanism can be fairly understood in the

context of the way of living.

a. The Maternity Principle
Maternity is understood as the source of life, the symbol of love and care. The one who gives birth to life, takes care of life, etc. is regarded as mother. Heaven, earth, country, sea, land, female and male... all are regarded as mother due to the function of begetting life, giving, fostering, and taking care of the life of clan, race, country, etc. The highest God, the creator of heaven and earth, is expressed in terms of Dao or the mother of all things."[10]

b. The Reasonable
Life comes out of union, and happy life is achieved by harmonious union. So, harmony (*hòa*/和) and union (*hợp*/合) are taken as the most reasonable way of living.[11] Reasonable is judged from the actual state of harmonious union of emotion and reason, reality and ideality (*hợp tình hợp lý*/合情合理), the means and the end, the effect and the consequence, etc. Being on good terms with nature (*thuận kỳ tự nhiên*/順其自然) and with fellow men (*dĩ hòa vi quý*/已和為貫) is living in accordance with the principle of reasonableness.

c. The Logic of the Heart (*tâm đạo*/心道)
Harmony is felt by heart, so living harmoniously means living in accordance with its rules. The logic of the heart works in two ways as the "good conscience" (lương tâm/良心), and as the common sense. Most of customs, traditions, rites are constructed from the common sense, i.e. from the heart of the people.

d. Union as the Way
Union consists of three steps: acknowledging the presence of different lives, uniting them harmoniously, and making them becoming a new life. It happens the way of how horizons are fused into a broader, more beautiful and more encompassing horizon.[12]

e. Theistic Humanism
Emphasis on the co-operative role of man in the process of life making

and cultivation of mutual and personal relationship with God and nature clearly indicate a kind of theistic humanism.[13]

f. Pluralistic Thinking, Inclusiveness and Syncretism
Since life is the ultimate end, and its growth or shrink is determined by many factors, the Viet are open for all ways or means which are helpful for life. However, such a pluralism is rational in the sense that these factors are classified according to their impact on life. God is the highest in ranking for his role as the life-giver, while the mercy-goddess (*quan Âm*/觀音) is the most beloved for her gentle role as life caretaker.

g. God in the Mind and Heart of the Viet
To the Viet, God is inseparable from life. They feel, see, hear and touch God in his many roles: life-giving, life-generating, life-saving, life-helping, life-bettering, life-comforting, and so on. He is referred to as emperor, king, ancestor, master, father, mother, brother, teacher and friend. He is personally called as "*Ông Trời*" (Mr. Heaven).[14] *Trời*, originally means a sphere above the earth, is personalized and worshipped as a good, just and benevolent immortal person. He is immanent and transcendent, in the world and out of the world, above us and in us, the named (道) and the unnamed (無). As life-giver, caretaker, judge, and comforter, *ÔngTrời* is present in their heart and mind. People who do good for the others, the people of moral and intellectual integrity, and the people of wisdom and heroic life are venerated as the men or women of God, i.e. gods, goddesses, saints, sages, heroes.[15]

Concluding Remarks: Vietnamese Theology in the Making
The Catholic Church of Vietnam is well known for its absolute loyalty to the Roman Catholic Church and its unconditional "filial piety" to the vicar of Christ. Theological teaching in priest-seminaries and convents is simply a mere repetition of theology approved by Rome; and theological research seems to be "luxurious" for pastoral ministry.[16] That explains an apparent lack of theological research despite abundant vocation, talents and interest.[17]

Such view on theology is changing. The promotion of inculturation of Vatican II, on the one side, and the unfriendly "no-religion" policy of

Vietnam, on the opposite side, are pushing the Vietnamese Catholic Church to find a way that satisfies both the mother Church and the mother Country. The Church is facing a heavy task of working out a theology that: (1) can disperse the long established bias against Christianity as an estranged, colonial, imperialist, reactionary and harmful religion to Vietnam; (2) that would facilitate the process of incarnation of Christianity in Vietnam, making it an inseparable part of the Viet-body; (3) and that Christianity could be accepted as a mother *ex aequo* with the country mother.

In a word, Vietnamese theology is a theology-of-and-for-life. Since God is life, and since life cannot be detached from the way and the truth (John 14:6), all ways of and to life are to be taken into theological consideration. As the source of life, maternity is the manifestation of deity. Motherhood expresses the feeling at home, i.e. the feeling of resting in mother's womb, the feeling of being nurtured, educated, fully communicated[18] and, above all, the feeling of belonging to the loved ones.[19] As such, motherhood means more than citizenship, partisanship or denominationalism.[20] It cannot be dogmatically restricted. It is in this sense that the Viet refer to God as *Ông Trời,* and to their country as mother.

For such theology, Vietnamese theologians begin with a retrieval of maternal values hidden in customs, traditions, thought and culture (*Kim Định* and *VũĐình Trác*)[21], and then continues with a fusion of Christian values into them, giving theology a Vietnamese face and a Christian soul (Peter C. Phan). Theology-of-and-for-life presents the Christian God as a Viet mother. As a mother, Christianity is taking care of her poor, underprivileged, oppressed, homeless, minority children.[22] No longer foreign in one's own country, Christianity as mother has to take Vietnam with its culture and way of living as her home.[23] It is in this sense that Vietnamese theology is a process of fighting for life and for being accepted as Vietnamese.

Notes

1. David Mungello, ed., *The Chinese Rites Controversy: Its History and Meaning* (Nettelal: Steyler, 1994).
2. That was the fate of Matteo Ricci's accommodation strategy. Accepted by Alexandre VII (1656), rejected by Clement XI (1704), petitioned by Jesuit missionaries, it was banned (*Ex illa die*, 1715), and forbidden by Benedict XIV (*Ex quo singular*, 1742).
3. Fu Pei-Jung, 'Chinese Thought and Christianity', *Collectanea Theologica* (Taipei: Kuang Chi,1978), p. 215.

4. Wolfgang Bauer, *China and the Search for Happiness: Recurring Themes in Four Thousand Years of Chinese Cultural History* (New York: Seabury Press, 1976). Trans. by Michael Shaw.
5. See Albert B. Chang, Dann sind Himmel und Menschen in Einheit, *Bautsteineeinerchinesischer Theologie* (Freiburg: Herder,1984), pp. 70-74.
6. Albert Chang, op. cit.; Gabriel Ly, *Man and God*, 9 Vols. (Taipei: Fujen University Press, 1985-2008). See also Tran van Doan, 'Ueberlegungenzueinerasiatischen Theologie', *ZeitschriftfuerMissionswissenschaft und Religionswissenschaft* (1986),Vol. 2/3, pp. 172-179.
7. Inner way and outer way are expressed by Wang Yang Ming as "Sageliness within, kingliness without" (內聖外王).
8. Martin Heidegger, *Identity and Difference* (1957) (New York: Harper Row, 1968). Trans. Joan Stambaugh.
9. TrânNgọc Thêm, *Tìm về bản sắc văn hóaViệt Nam: Cái nhìn hệ thống – loại hình* (Hochiminh City: HCM Publishing House, 2004), pp. 75-93.
10. Lao Tse, *Tao Te King*, 1: 'The Name is the mother of all things' (萬物之母).
11. Tran van Doan, *Reason, Rationality, Reasonableness* (Washington DC: The Council for Research in Values and Philosophy, 2000).
12. Hans-Georg Gadamer, *Wahrheit und Method* (Tubingen: Mohr, 1960), pp. 289-290.
13. Kim Định, *CửaKhổng* (Saigon: Ra Khơi, 1961), pp. 93-124.
14. The Viet invoke the name of God as *Thiên Chúa* (天主), *Chúa* (主), *Thượng Đế* (上帝) (in the Chinese tradition), but most common as *Trời* (Heaven), *Chúa Trời* (Lord on Heaven), *ÔngTrời* (Mr. Heaven), and *Thầy Chí thánh* (Holy Teacher).
15. A common practice among popular religions like Caodaism, Hòa Hảo Buddhism, and Bahá'í. See Trần Ngọc Thêm, op. cit., pp. 234-255.
16. Almost all theological works in Vietnam are textbooks or translated works. Well-known are Phan Tấn Thành (a former professor at Angelicum in Rome) and Nguyễn Văn Trinh (a professor at the St. Joseph Priest Seminary), the two most productive authors.
17. With ca. 7-8 million followers (ca. 7.2% of population), over 5000 priests, over 5000 seminarians and students and 33.097 religious men and women (2019), the Church did not have any research institute or review specialising in theology, for political reason, until recent years. *Hợp Tuyển Thần Học* (Collecta Theologica), is republished by the Jesuit College (Thủ Đức), and the already closed review *Triết Đạo*, a research review of philosophy and theology, are to be named here.
18. Hans-Georg Gadamer, *Wahrheit und Method*, op. cit., pp.7-38.
19. Peter C. Phan, *Being Religious Interreligious – Asian Perspectives on Interfaith Dialogue* (Maryknoll, NY: Orbis Book, 2004), pp. 60-84. See also Aloysius Pieris, *Love Meets Wisdom – A Christian Experience of Buddhism* (Maryknoll, NY: Orbis Books, 1988); Raimon Panikkar, *The Intra-Religious Dialogue* (New York: Paulist Press, 1999).
20. Hans Kueng & Julia Ching, *Christentum und Chinesische Religion* (Muenchen-Zurich: Piper, 1988), pp. 303-07.
21. Kim Định, *Việt Lý Tố Nguyên* (Saigon: An Tiêm, 1971); Vũ Đình Trác, *Triết Lý Nhân Bản Nguyễn Du* (Orange: Hội Hữu, 1988).
22. A mild form of theology of liberation is seen in the works of Nguyễn Thái Hợp, former bishop of Vinh and Hà Tĩnh, and professor at Angelicum in Rome, and Vũ Kim Chính, a Jesuit and professor at Fujen University.
23. Theology of inculturation is the main current at Học Viện Công Giáo Việt Nam (Institut Catholique du Vietnam), established in 2015 by the Catholic Bishops' Conference of Vietnam with Archbishop Bùi Văn Đọc (1944-2018), a noted theologian, as great chancellor and Bishop Đinh Đức Đạo, a former professor at Urban University in Rome, as its first president.

Biblical Interpretation in India from Subaltern Perspectives

ANTONY JOHN BAPTIST

India has a long tradition of interpreting the Bible. This tradition can be reduced to two kinds of theologies: i. culture and religion based inculturation, and ii. socio-economic based liberation. In the post Independent Era and the post Second Vatican Council times, the first one evolved to establish theological equality of the Eastern and Indian traditions with the West. Hindu religious texts, traditions, theologies and practices were studied or compared with the Christian ones. In the process it discarded or excluded the subaltern as 'small or little traditions'. Inculturation theology in India was selective and elitist, limited to upper middle and urbanized class of people, but presenting it as pan-Indian culture. In reaction to this, in the seventies and eighties of the last century, drawing inspiration from Liberation theology, which sees poverty as result of structural injustice, concentration to the poor became important and predominant.

This article studies Biblical interpretation in India from the subaltern perspective in two parts. The first one situates Biblical interpretation in the history and context of Indian theology. The second one presents some of the trends that are found in the subaltern interpretation of Bible such as i. Victimhood to subjecthood, ii. Asserting agency and working out destiny, and iii. From being objects to subjects.

Introduction

In India, exegetical and hermeneutical studies of Sacred Scriptures have a long tradition. As far as Biblical interpretations are concerned, the contribution of William Carey, the well-known Baptist missionary of the early 19th century, is monumental. For the Catholic tradition, the Second

Biblical Interpretation in India from Subaltern Perspectives

Vatican Council and its document *Dei Verbum* gave a new impetus and paved way for varieties of Biblical activities. There have been different attempts to translate the Bible into various languages of this great nation, rich in languages and cultures, and to distribute it. Different associations such as The Society for Biblical Studies in India (SBSI), The Catholic Association of India (CBAI), The Bible Society of India (BSI) and various church bodies continue to do tremendous work in this regard. On these grounds, new and community-oriented interpretations of the Bible could arise, in particular 'Subaltern Indian Biblical Interpretation' from a Dalit perspective. In a first step I will give a quick survey of the colonial heritage of Biblical Interpretation, then of post-colonial attempts to read the Bible, and in a second step I want to present some of the trends in Subaltern, specifically Dalit, Biblical Interpretation.

I. Situating the Subaltern Perspective of Biblical Interpretation

In line with R. Sugirtharajah, Biblical interpretation in India can be grouped as *colonial* and *post-colonial*. He classifies very neatly the colonial interpretations into three modes: "Orientalist", "Anglicist", and "Nativist".[1]

1. Colonial Interpretations
1.1 The Orientalist Mode[2]

The Orientalists attempted to study India's ancient linguistic, philosophical and religious heritage, elevating Sanskrit to high status. They interpreted the Bible demonstrating the similarities between Biblical and Vedic texts. This school attempts to construct the inner and mystical meaning of the texts. In this line some speak of inter-textual study of comparing Bible with other sacred scriptures of India, as reading the Bible through Indian eyes that will give an authentically Indian interpretation.

Assessing this approach Selva Rathinam, an Indian Biblical Scholar, remarks:

> ... the Orientalists' uncritical equation of India with Hindu-Aryan not only neglected the vernacular, the native and folk traditions, the materialistic and theistic Lokayata and Sankhya systems and Islamic and Persian influences but also left unexamined the damage done to the Dalits and the tribal peoples. This Orientalist hermeneutics created

a spiritual Hindu India and offered very little to alleviate the plight of the poor."[3]

1.2. The Anglicist Mode
While these attempts were done in popular, pastoral and ashramite circles, in the institutes of higher learning of both Catholic and Protestant circles, the application of Historical Critical Method was used as the method of Biblical interpretation. The Anglicist Mode introduced Western modes of Biblical investigation in Indian theological colleges. The "Indian Church Commentary", initiated during the colonial era, and "The Christian Student's Library", written soon after Indian independence are some of the examples.[4]

However, George M. Soares-Prabhu, assessing it from Asian and Indian perspective, argued that it is ineffective, irrelevant and ideologically loaded because of the vested interests: "It is concerned only with the informational elements of the text, deliberately abstracting from its emotive resonances and its practical implications."[5] Further he opines that, "a Western style exegesis, ... is thrust down the throats of bewildered third world students, living among starving, oppressed, largely non-Christian masses - whose concern seldom figure in our text books!"[6]

1.3 The Nativistic Mode
The Nativistic mode has searched for models in the vernacular tradition. This has offered an alternative to classical culture in languages other than Sanskrit and paved the way for a shift from a Vedantic to a Bhakti type of religious experience.[7] In this mode, the hermeneutical enterprise is governed by rules set by a particular language and culture.

2. Authentic Indian Biblical Interpretation
Amid these interpretations and exegetical exercises in India, there have been repeated questions on what is 'Indian', and 'Indianness' about Indian Biblical Interpretations. Much has been pointed out, of which two aspects stand as special to Indian context: its multifaceted religiosity with multiplicity of religious traditions and its massive poverty with the oppressive Caste System which is common to South Asia too. Corresponding to these two realities of India, Soares Prabhu proposed

an integral Indian Reading, comprising of 'religious' reading and 'social' reading. They are complementary to each other and enrich each other.

3. Postcolonial Indian Biblical Interpretations

Among the numerous aspects of postcolonial criticism, I will highlight the following: it brings marginal elements or voices which have been subjected to institutional and exegetical forgetting in the text to the front and, in the process, subverts the traditional meaning. It looks in the text for oppositional or protest voices. Instead of blaming the victims, postcolonial reading will direct attention to the social structures and institutions which spawn victimhood.[8] A postcolonial interpretation of the Bible also comes as a corrective to uncritical adaptation of Eurocentrism. It addresses the questions which affect people's lives. The purpose of its reading is not so much to produce subtle nuances of emotion and feeling in individuals but to help communities to face the problems of the contemporary world where people are thrown together more and more in multilingual, multiracial, and multifaith societies. However, it does not romanticize or idealize the poor.

However, one must distinguish the postmodern, anti-colonial and postcolonial approaches. Postmodernism, for example, makes room for varied interpretations but postcolonialism makes an option for a particular way of looking at and reading the text. Anti-colonial movements have rarely represented the interests of all the subaltern peoples of a colonized country. The dismantling of colonial rule did not automatically bring about changes for the better in the status of women, the working class, the Dalits and the tribals.

In the postcolonial era, two factors contributed to emphasizing the subaltern perspective in Indian Biblical interpretation: Liberation Theology and New Methods of Biblical Interpretation. The arrival of Liberation Theology from Latin American countries, though criticized for using Marxian social analysis, without including caste axis, gave a push to and a methodology to read Bible from below, from the perspective of the poor and the marginalized.

In India at first it was the YCW (Young Christian Workers) and the student movements that took up this way of reading the text. Then it was picked up by the seminaries, theologians and exegetes. According to L. Legrand, South American liberation theology was the result of praxis of the struggling communities which were later articulated by exegetes and theologians. But in India it was first the professionally trained theologians and exegetes who formulated ideas of Liberation Theology which were later tried or brought to people whose reading of the Bible was otherwise predominantly pietistic and individualistic.[9]

New methods of literary analysis and approaches that used human sciences and especially a sociological approach were recognized by the Pontifical Biblical Commission in the document 'The Interpretation of the Bible in the Church'. This also allowed Indian Biblical interpretation to go beyond Historical Critical Methods. The Contextual Approaches, such as the Liberationist and Feminist approaches, and the Reader-Response theories, brought the reader to the centre and his/her concerns and struggles as part of exegetical exercises. Using the model of the "fusion of horizons" of Gadamer, new dialogues between the text and the reader were set in motion where new meanings emerged for the liberation of the subalterns. Unlike the Western approach of Reader-Response theories where the reader approaches the text as an individual, for the Subaltern, both Asian and South American, reading and interpretation of the Bible is a communitarian exercise for their emancipation and liberation.[10]

4. Biblical Interpretation from a Subaltern Perspective

It is at the juncture of Indian Biblical scholarship that one has to situate Biblical interpretation from subaltern perspectives. Though the dictionary meaning of subaltern is 'of inferior rank', it generally refers to subordination, in terms of class, caste, age, gender and office. In the Indian and South Asian context, it might point in more specific way to Dalit men and women. In other words, in the Indian context, it consciously refers to the people suffering still under the hegemony of caste system.[13]

Since the later part of last century many researches, monographs, and exegetical works have been undertaken from the perspectives of Dalits in general and Dalit women in particular, both in Protestant and Catholic circles, and they are still continuing. In the next section, I attempt to mention only three of the salient trends of exegesis and researches that are done from subaltern, Dalit, perspectives.

II. Some Trends in Subaltern Interpretations of the Bible in India

Biblical Interpretation in India from Subaltern Perspectives

At the beginning of Indian subaltern Biblical interpretation, the Exodus event attracted the attention of exegetes. There were comparisons between slavery in Egypt and caste in India, the poor in the Bible and Dalits as poor. The ministry of Jesus was seen as a ministry to the poor. In all these, the victimhood of Dalit men and women was emphasized rather than their agency. They were seen as poor and suffering, to be pitied and ministered to. In the recent past, however, Biblical interpretations from subaltern perspective have moved beyond this to include themes such as subjecthood, identity, self-dignity, self-assertion etc.[14] In the following section, based on a Dalit feminist reading of three characters of the Old Testament, namely Hagar (Gen 16), Tamar (Gen 38:1-27) and the unnamed Concubine of the Levite (Judg 19), I attempt to pinpoint three characteristics of this progress.

1. From Victimhood to Subjecthood
Deviating from the earlier subaltern Biblical studies that portrayed the Dalits as victims of the caste system, patriarchal violence, and economic deprivation, and finding parallels in the Biblical worlds and texts, of late, the researches have come to record their own subjecthood.

In my own research on Hagar (Gen 16) and Dalit women, I have attempted to present them as ones asserting their subjecthood. At the point of pregnancy (Gen 16:4), Hagar came to an awareness of her new status as wife of Abraham and mother of the child. This "evoked her vision of equality and mutuality towards Sarai. ...This interiorization brought about a sense of self-worth, which was dormant in her."[15] Again in v. 8, in response to the messenger of God when she was fleeing from her mistress, "She registers her claims, arguments, her protest and her perception of the situation."[16] The character of Ishmael also becomes an example of asserting his subjecthood: "He would be a free man, free from social constraints, independent like the nomadic tribes of the desert. ... He will not be dominated or domesticated, ... he will not be a slave to any one, ... he will be free in the desert."[17] So Hagar and Ishmael stand as models for Dalit men and women of the present time. They are not silent sufferers of the caste system and patriarchy, but persons who assert their subjecthood. Vinothraj Amaladass, a Dalit scholar, calls for a Dalit theology that will "give birth to a new person called dalit-self – liberated, inclusive and dignified – who is capable of leading the Indian society and the church into new pathways."[18]

2. Asserting Agency and Working out their own Destiny

The subalterns are no more the passive recipients of oppression and subjugation. Now, they exercise their agency and work out their own destiny. Though they are aware that any sign of protest and opposition to the existing system could bring 'greater oppression' and annihilate or wipe them out, subalterns, both Dalit men and women, at times take up overt or covert forms of resistance. Some of the minor characters of the Bible serve as inspiration.

Hagar, at the oppression of Sarai, chose to run away from Abraham's house (Gen 16:6). This decision reveals her scale of values. As Elsa Tamez points out, "Hagar had rejected her slavery. She was not interested in trying to win Sarah's good will by suffering the abuses in silence. *Hagar preferred to die in the desert.*"[19] She takes command of her own life and works out her own liberation. This shows her will for freedom. Though Dalits, such as Hagar, know that they will be 'in crisis' yet they 'create crisis'. They take up all the measures possible to work out their own destiny.

Anderson Jeremiah, studying the Tamar story (Gen 38:6-30) from a Dalit women's perspective, sees it as reclaiming 'her' rights. Tamar uses her sexuality to claim her status and security. She takes the matter in her own hands and her action is a rebellion against the authority and custom of her time. Realization of their existential situation and determination are the two aspects that join Tamar and Dalit women in their search for liberation. On Dalit woman, Anderson comments, "No longer had she to passively accept the degradation and grinding poverty but fight against her husband, family and the patriarchal society through which man exercises his authority and power."[20] Thus Tamar provides a paradigm.

In the Levite's Concubine narrative, the unnamed concubine apparently plays no active role, but only a passive one. As was the custom of her time, she is not an acting subject, but an acted upon object. She was never consulted either at her home (Judg 19:1-10), on turning aside to Gibeah (vv. 11-15) or when the Levite decided to throw her out (v. 25). However, Arisapogu Sam Thomas sees Hermeneutics of Resistance in the very words of v. 27, the half verse that states, "There was his concubine lying at the door of the house, with her hands on the threshold." Firstly, the body of the concubine, though silent, becomes the agent of resistance, exposing the atrocities of violence against her (v. 30). Her body cut into twelve pieces, limb by limb, sent throughout the territory of Israel, provoked the Israelites to take action against suspects. Secondly, her hands on the threshold speak of her last resort for safety and protection. By reaching out to the threshold, she voiced out or attempted to communicate her right to freedom. It is a symbol of her resistance. Applying this to women in general and Dalit women in particular whose bodies are tormented, raped, abused, Sam Thomas asserts that their bodies can become a weapon to fight against the unjust society which is structured by caste and patriarchal dominance.[21]

3. From Being Objects to be Subjects
For too long, the academia has treated subalterns as *objects* of study and not as *subjects*. But now a good number of Dalit men and Dalit women have become subjects of study, including Biblical studies. However, it must be admitted that the presence of Dalit women in Biblical study is very rare.[22] Felix Wilfred names it as an 'academic agency of the marginalized', which paves the way for their inclusion. Any research done on them by others may not bring out the way they experience life. Only when subalterns become subjects of study will their specific contribution be brought in. Otherwise, the intellectual community and society will be deprived of it and will remain incomplete and impoverished. Their contribution would help to correct and to re-orient the believing and secular community in the right direction.[23] This Biblical study is not for 'enlightenment' of mind but for enabling life, life in abundance (cf. John 10:10).

Notes

1. Cf. R. S. Sugirtharajah, *Asian Biblical Hermeneutics and Postcolonialism*, Sheffield: Sheffield Academic Press, 1999, 3.
2. Orientalists are those who initiated the scholarly study of India's ancient sacred and other texts. Thus, making Indians to be proud of their own history and heritage. The Orientalist Biblical Scholars attempted to i. study the parallels between Indian texts and the Bible, and ii. use Indian methods such as the Nyaya, the Vaisesika and the Sankhya to interpret Biblical texts.
3. Selva Rathinam, 'Postcolonial Biblical Interpretation for India', in Mathew Jayanath (ed.), *Indian Theologies of Methods and Models for Theologizing*, Pune: Jnana-Deepa Vidyapeeth, 2017, 59-83, here 68. Also cf. Sugirtharajah, *Asian Biblical Hermeneutics*,129-139; Vinothraj Amaladass, *Breaking Pyramid: A Dalit-Self's New Humanity*, Delhi: ISPCK, 2020, 294- 302 for a Dalit's critique of inculturation.
4. Cf. Selva Rathinam, 'Postcolonial Biblical Interpretation for India', 69.
5. G. M. Soares Prabhu, 'Towards an Indian Interpretation of the Bible', in Isaac Padinjarekuttu (ed.), *Biblical Themes for a Contextual Theology Today: Collected Writings of George M. Soares-Prabhu*, vol.

1, Pune: Jnana-Deepa Vidhyapeeth, 1999, 207-222, here 211.
6. G. M. Soares Prabhu, 'Towards an Indian Interpretation of the Bible', 212.
7. Vedanta is one of the six astika schools of Hindu Philosophy. The Bhakti movement refers to the trend that was brought forward by a number of Hindu saints in medieval Hinduism who sought to bring religious reforms by adopting the method of devotion to achieve salvation.
8. Cf. Sugirtharajah, *Asian Biblical Hermeneutics*, 22-23.
9. Cf. Lucien Legrand, 'Twenty Years of Biblical Renewal in India', in A. Aloysius Xavier, P. Joseph Titus (eds.), *The Word is Near You: Collected Papers of Lucien Legrand MEP*, vol. 3, Bangalore: St. Peter's Pontifical Institute, 2004, 29- 42, here 38.
10. Cf. Antony John Baptist, *Together as Sisters: Hagar and Dalit Women*, Delhi: ISPCK, 2012, 20-21; *Unsung Melodies from Margins*, Delhi: ISPCK, 2014, 122-123; Hans-Georg Gadamer, *Truth and Method*, London: Sheed& Ward, 1975.
11. Dalits are the people who are considered by the Brahminical social order as the lowest in the caste system. In fact, they are called by many caste names and in the Government records they are termed as Scheduled Castes (SC). Dalit is the name that they have given to themselves as mark of their identity and dignity.
12. If Dalits are the lowest in the braminical social order, Dalit women are the lowest. They are thrice discriminated in terms of caste, class and gender: Dalits among Dalits.
13. Cf. Ranajit Guha, 'Preface' in Ranajit Guha (ed.), *Subaltern Studies: Writings on South Asian History and Society*, vol. 1, New Delhi: Oxford University Press, 1982, vii-viii, here vii.
14. To name some examples: Antony John Baptist, 'Together as Sisters: Hagar and Dalit Women in Exercising their Agency', *Jeevadhara* 41, no.241 (Jan 2011), 56-65; Anderson Jeremiah, 'Reclaiming 'Her' Right: Rereading the Story of Tamar (Genesis 38:1-27) from Dalit women Perspective', *Bangalore Theological Forum* 38, no.1 (June 2006), 145-156; Arisapogu Sam Thomas, 'Reinterpreting the Narrative of the Concubine in Judges 19 for Dalit Women's Liberation: Towards their Empowerment and Implications for the Engagement of the Church', *Bangalore Theological Forum* 52, no. 2 (December 2020), 177-195; S. John, 'The Lamenting God: A Postcolonial Juxtaposition of Lament in the Book of Lamentations and Select Dalit Literature', *Bangalore Theological Forum* 49, no. 2 (December, 2017), 133- 153; K. Jesurathnam, 'Dalit and Subaltern Hermeneutics in Conversation with Reader Response Method: 1 Kings 22, A Case in Point', *Bangalore Theological Forum* 48, no. 1 (June 2016), 46- 60; Jeeva Kumar Ravela, '"The Lord Forbid that I should give you my Land": Land Rights in 1 Kings 21 and its Implication to the Land Rights of Dalits', *Bangalore Theological Forum* 43, no. 1 (June 2011), 121-147.
15. John Baptist, *Together as Sisters*, 111. So also in the Tamar narrative: Tamar decides to take her own steps to gain her right back. The realization / interiorization of her existential situation plays a crucial role as the beginning of the liberation process. The subalterns need to realize that they have the right to reclaim the identity and equality that has been denied to them, and that they have a right to oppose the victimization at the hands of patriarchal caste system. (cf. Anderson Jeremiah, 'Reclaiming 'Her' Right', 151.)
16. John Baptist, *Together as Sisters*, 134 (emphasis by the author).
17. John Baptist, *Together as Sisters*, 148.
18. Vinothraj Amaladass, *Breaking Pyramid*, xi.
19. Elsa Tamez, 'The Woman who Complicated the History of Salvation', *Cross Currents* 36, no.2 (1986), 129-139, here 133, emphasis added.
20. Anderson Jeremiah, 'Reclaiming 'Her' Right', 152.
21. Cf. Sam Thomas, 'Reinterpreting the Narrative', 187.
22. It is because in India, Christian Biblical studies and theology, still, remains a requirement for the formation of priests and pastors and no Dalit women, laity or religious, can easily become a faculty member in the seminaries and faculties. Dalit women still need to become a strong voice and 'Subjects' of Biblical studies.
23. Cf. Felix Wilfred, *Theology for an Inclusive World*, Delhi: ISPCK, 2019, 270-271.

Part Three: Asian Questions and Approaches to Christian Ethics

Catholic Theological Ethics in Asia: From Conflict to Conversation

MARIA JOHN P. SELVAMANI

The Catholic Church is one of the leading healthcare providers in Asia. Yet, the Church finds itself in conflict with public health policies that are incompatible with Catholic teachings. This paper, taking the response of the Catholic Bishops' Conference of Taiwan to the Patient Right to Autonomy Act as an example, argues that moral theological discussions in Asia need to take place in the context of the presence of vibrant ancient cultures, philosophies and religions, instead of from a dogmatic standpoint. This paper further suggests that the Catholic Church in Asia needs to open itself to the challenges posed by the wider society and be willing to dialogue and discern on ethical issues within the Church as well as with other religions, and society at large.

1. Introduction

Catholic theological ethics is facing challenges both internally and externally. The relationship between theological and secular ethics is at risk, due to lack of interest from theologians to engage in public discourse and a suspicion of theologians among the secular ethicists.[1] The right to autonomy in the field of secular ethics is in conflict with the protection of human dignity from conception to death in Catholic theological ethics, leading to a war between "culture of life" and "culture of death".

In Asia, the Catholic Church, though a minority, has substantial influence on all aspects of the society through its educational, social and healthcare institutions. The church in Asia too faces a society that is increasingly secular and is being challenged by various public policies that are not compatible with Catholic teaching. In such situations, the Church, in addition to opposing such public policies, often refuses to comply with them. This paper uses the response of the Chinese Regional Bishops' Conference of Taiwan to the Patient Right to Autonomy Act as an example, and suggests that there is a need for wider dialogue and discernment on ethical issues within the Catholic Church, and with other religions and society at large.

2. Catholic Response to Patient Right to Autonomy Act in Taiwan[2]

Taiwan is already at the verge of becoming a super-aged society in which one in five persons is above sixty-five years of age. As a society that values filial piety, there is socio-cultural pressure to keep the elderly alive at all cost, which has made Taiwan a land of respirators with more than twenty thousand patients on respirators and 70-80% of these being unconscious.[3] End of life situations are often prone to conflict between the healthcare professionals and the family of the patients, especially when the patients are unconscious. In recent decades, respect for the patient's autonomy has become the most important principle of medical ethics. To ensure respect for patient autonomy, to protect the right of patients to a good and natural death, and to promote a harmonious relationship between physicians and patients, the Patient Right to Autonomy Act (PAA) was promulgated on January 6, 2016. It came into effect on January 6, 2019.[4] This Act encourages citizens to sign an advance directive on end of life care after sessions of advance care planning. Under this Act, one can sign an advance directive to accept or refuse any life sustaining treatment, including artificial nutrition and hydration when one is terminally ill, in an irreversible coma, in persistent vegetative state, suffering from severe dementia and other conditions in which one is in intolerable suffering due to an incurable disease for which no appropriate treatment options are available.[5] This Act also offers the option to designate a healthcare agent who will be responsible for end of life care decisions. The advance directive will be implemented only after the patient's condition is assessed by two physicians with relevant expertise, and confirmed in at least two meetings convened by the palliative team. This Act is proudly presented as the first in Asia and people are being encouraged in the public media to sign an advance directive with the slogan "My Life, My Decision".[6] More than 25,000 people have signed their advance directive under the PAA.[7]

The Catholic Church has opposed this Act from the beginning, and regards it as a legalization of indirect euthanasia. The official statement from the Chinese Regional Bishops Conference published in the *Catholic Weekly* on May 24, 2020, states that all the available options violate the teachings of the Church, so Catholics are advised not to sign an advance directive under this Act. The main argument is that the PAA legally allows for the refusal of artificial nutrition and hydration which, according to Catholic teaching, is indirect euthanasia. It contends that providing nutrition and hydration, even by artificial means, is basic care, and it cannot be refused or denied.

The concern of the Church that PAA opens the door to euthanasia is understandable. Other scholars also have pointed to the flaws and the limitations in the implementation of the Act in actual clinical settings.[8] But, not permitting the Catholics to sign an advance directive is not reasonable. It is true that St. Pope John Paul II and the Congregation for the Doctrine of the Faith have clearly stated that nutrition and hydration, though surgically administered, is necessary and obligatory.[9] But, it should be noted that these statements were made in the context of persistent vegetative state patients and not necessarily applicable to the other conditions listed in the PAA. Research shows that the potential benefits of tube feeding do not outweigh the associated burden for the persons with advanced dementia, one of the clinical conditions listed in this Act. So, hand feeding is recommended as long as possible.[10] The main aim of PAA is to enable people to express their values and preferences for end of life care, and be assured that these will be respected.

The Church's teaching on the end of life decisions is very clear. While defending the obligation to respect and care for one's life till the end, prolonging life at any cost is not advocated. Traditionally, this tension was resolved using an assessment of "ordinary and extraordinary" treatment, which is a benefit or burden analysis from the patient's point of view. This assessment considers the totality of a person's life situation, rather than whether one is terminally ill, or near death. So, if artificial nutrition and hydration becomes a burden rather than a benefit, as may occur for a person with advanced dementia, it can be refused considering the totality of the person's life. The Church's concern for persons who are particularly vulnerable, who may be abandoned at the end of life without basic care of hydration and nutrition, is justifiable. But, by advising Catholics not to sign an advance directive, the Church restricts the autonomy of Catholics in expressing their values and wishes on end of life care. Moreover, it implies that by signing an advance directive on end of life care, following PAA, Catholics are consenting to euthanasia. For the aged Catholic population, such a directive from the Bishops does not provide comfort. Without such an advance directive, elderly Catholics have no other official forum to express their healthcare preferences. They are not even allowed to designate someone as their healthcare agent. Apart from the statement of the Bishops there has been no further public discussion on PAA among the Catholics in Taiwan.

3. A Way Forward for Catholic Theological Ethics in Asia

As the above discussion reveals, the Catholic Church in Asia, faced with legislation that is not consistent with Catholic teaching, often expresses its opposition through an internal statement, and advises the Catholics and Catholic institutions to claim conscientious objection and not to participate. In countries like the Philippines, being a majority, the Church tends to use its strength to influence public policy.[11] Catholic theological ethics has very strong philosophical and theological foundations that can enrich the modern society in its deliberations on ethics. But by refusing to dialogue, theological ethics in Asia is becoming increasingly irrelevant. As the working document of the Taiwan Evangelization Congress acknowledges, the great challenge to the Church is the secularized culture that promotes values and legislation that are in contrast with the Gospel and the Church's teaching. It is also recognized that the way the Church in Taiwan has responded to various issues has led to a certain amount of dissatisfaction within the Church and caused confusion among Catholics.

The moral theological discussions in Asia need to take place in the context of vibrant ancient cultures, philosophies, and religions. Plurality of cultural and religious practices and philosophical thinking is the foundational experience of Asians. Dialogue has therefore been the primary method of evangelization in the history of the Catholic Church in Asia. The recognition that the cultures and religions of Asia indeed express the noblest longings of the people, and have profound spiritual and ethical meaning and values, has been the experience of many foreign missionaries who have ever touched Asian soil. However challenging it may be, the present situation invites the Church to dialogue within itself, and with other religions and related professional, scientific and academic circles on values that are important to society and the Church.

3.1. Dialogue within the Church

Since most parts of Asia have been evangelized by Western missionaries, the Catholic Church in Asia is generally viewed as a foreign religion. Recognizing that Asian Catholics live their faith within the Hindu-Buddhist-Taoist-Confucian cultural context, many local festivals and customs have been adapted into the liturgical celebrations. But similar integration has not taken place in moral theology. The tension between the ethical norms of the Church and the lived realities of Asian Catholics continues to exist. Catholic theological ethics is predominantly based on the Greco-Roman philosophical system, which cannot be adequately translated into the Asian cultural ethos. For an Asian mind, moral norms are not directives to be obeyed, but orientations to be interpreted. This might lead to ambiguity in the application of moral norms, but for the Asian *yin-yang* culture, ambiguity is part of life experience, which needs to be harmonized.[12] In this framework, universal norms are not the only basis of moral decisions. A person's duties in social relationships also play a key role.

Given this cultural context, the Catholic Church in Asia needs to focus on the conscience building of its faithful. This cannot be done by merely providing a list of rules that Catholics should comply with, but by conversing with the lived realities of the people. It is not enough for the Church in Asia to be only a dispenser of doctrinal norms, but it should also be an interlocutor in reflecting along with the faithful on the experiences, anxieties and questions they face.[13] As the Catholic Church in Asia continues to face conflicts over the ethical issues raised by homosexual unions, medically assisted reproduction, surrogacy and euthanasia, dialogue and discernment is needed within the Catholic Church. The dilemma one faces in caring for a loved one who suffers from dementia, or who is in permanent vegetative state, and the suffering of the terminally ill, of couples facing problems with infertility, and the pain of homosexuals needs to be listened to and acknowledged. This needs to be followed by a process of discernment in which the Church teachings are critically evaluated against these experiences of the people.

The content of the statement from the Bishops on PAA could have been different if there had been a dialogue with important stakeholders, including Catholics of advanced years and the Catholic proponents of the PAA. Bishops could have realized that, just like everyone else who has signed an advance directive, Catholics too wish to die with dignity and also do not want to leave end of life decisions to their family and do not want to be a social and economic burden.[14] As a result, even though they might have upheld the Catholic teaching on artificial nutrition and hydration, they might have acknowledged the positive aims of this Act and, at the least, approved Catholics to designate a healthcare agent, which is encouraged by the Catholic Church in other countries. At the moment, Catholics are left to their own conscience to decide on PAA.

In this dialogue, it is also important to encourage Asian theologians and Catholic professionals to openly discuss these morally controversial issues. In Asia, most of the faculties of theology are not affiliated with regular educational institutions. Besides, they tend to primarily focus on the training of future clergy and leaders of the Church. So, there is less opportunity for critical discussion. Theologians and clergy in these institutions at times face tacit demands not to discuss certain matters, or even offer opinions in public about controversial ethical issues. Those who do are reprimanded and even asked to publicly apologize. If the Church in Asia wants to play its role in modern Asian society, it needs to open itself to challenges with humility and show a willingness to learn from these challenges.

3.2. Dialogue with other religions

The strong presence of major world religions is one of the Asia's strengths. For Asians, religion is not a personal spirituality, but an integral part of one's identity. So, religious conversion, in some parts of Asia, is not change of religious affiliation, but change of one's identity and it will have far reaching consequences socially and culturally. Even secularism, for an Asian mind, is not necessarily a denial of religious belief, but an openness to all religious experiences. Religious plurality is one of the important realities of Asian society, and Catholic theological ethics cannot ignore it.

Though inter-religious dialogue has been an important characteristic of the mission of the Church in Asia, this has not led to deeper cooperation among religions on social and ethical issues. The Catholic Church in Asia, by working in tandem with other religious traditions, can make its concerns heard. In Taiwan, being a truly secular state in Asia, where no political or religious ideology dictates public policy, major religions can play an important role in advising society and government. Inter-religious dialogue on ethical issues in Asia can do a tremendous service to the society by ensuring that the public policies care for the welfare of the common people. Such a dialogue, is neither focused on convincing the other on the reasonableness of one's view, nor creating a uniform code. It is a process of searching together for solutions that will promote human flourishing both individually and collectively.[15] It is also challenging because it not only requires the Church to confront the ethical concepts of others, but to scrutinize its own concepts, which might call for a revision of Catholic traditional teachings.

In Taiwan, the Catholic Church is the only religion that has explicitly opposed PAA. While there is hardly any discussion on this Act among the other Christian Churches, the Buddhist scholars consider that as long as the intention is not to accelerate death, it is acceptable to refuse life sustaining treatments and artificial nutrition and hydration at a stage of one's sickness where there is a lack of quality of life.[16] If there could be an inter-religious and ecumenical dialogue on this issue, Catholic theological ethics may enlighten other religious groups on the flaws of this Act and, at the same time, the Church may accept that, under certain medical conditions it might be acceptable to refuse artificial nutrition and hydration. Such a dialogue will also ensure that this Act achieves its aim and does not slip into indirect euthanasia.

3.3. Dialogue with professionals and the public
The Covid-19 pandemic has revealed the inequality and injustice in the global healthcare system. In this situation, Catholic theological ethics has a prophetic role in building an equitable society. Catholic theological ethics is not just a discipline for clergy to study to administer the sacrament of reconciliation, but is also a system of ethical thinking.

In the West, theological ethics is viewed with suspicion by specialists in biomedical ethics. But in Asia, the Catholic Church is respected for its spirit of selfless service and integrity, and generally welcomed at the public policy discussions. As one of the leading healthcare providers in Asia, the Catholic Church can take the leadership to engage professionals and academics on modern ethical issues.

Though various aspects of PAA are still being discussed, the Catholic moral theologians have hardly taken part in discussion with the secular scholars or the public. When they did, it was to defend the official view of the Church. Catholic moral theology and Church's rich experience in caring for the sick, elderly and dying can provide much needed foundation on end of life care issues. Catholic moral theologians need to confidently converse with the secular scholars and the public. Instead of disputing over the ethical concepts, the Church can dialogue with others on the life concerns and experiences, on the anxieties and fears, and on the hopes and dreams of "ordinary people" because these are experiences that are common to everyone irrespective of their religious and political affiliation or social and economic status. Through its healthcare and social service institutions, Catholic Church in Asia is in touch the pulse of the society. This knowledge and experience of the Church can enhance the discussion. The Church also will be challenged by this dialogue, leading to confusion among Catholics on the teachings of the Church. As Pope Francis expects, the Church is to be bruised, hurting and dirty, rather than to be confined to its own quiet security.[17] The Church in Asia needs to be disturbed and shaken from its slumber. Catholic theological ethics in Asia should not be locked behind the walls of seminaries and churches. It needs to face the "danger" of the diversity of social and cultural values.

4. Conclusion

Using the example of the Catholic Church in Taiwan's response to PAA, this paper suggests that Catholic theological ethics in Asia needs to engage in dialogue within the Church, with other religious groups, with the academic community, and the public. The Catholic Church in Asia has the moral authority to advise society at large. Although the Church in Asia has, since Vatican II, developed its unique brand of theology in response to the context of Asian experience, there is nevertheless much to be done, especially in the field of theological ethics.

The statement of the Bishops on PAA reveals that the Church in Taiwan is still hesitant to converse with the wider society on sensitive issues such as end of life care. It is not sufficient for the Catholic Church in Asia to respond with a simplistic "yes" or "no" to healthcare legislation. It is of paramount importance for the Church to enter into dialogue with scientists and secular ethicists on the core concepts and structures of healthcare.

The Catholic Church in Asia, to fulfil its prophetic role, needs to open itself to the challenges from wider society. Catholic theological ethics needs to reinvent itself in the context of Asian experience. Just as the missionaries from the West who came to Asia realized that God is already alive in Asian cultures, it is important to realize that at the depth of everyone's conscience, there is a divine voice that guides them in the challenges of their life. Asia needs the Catholic Church to nurture people's conscience and accompany them as they pass through the vicissitudes of daily life.

Notes

1. Michael McCarthy, Mary Homan, and Michael Rozier, 'There Is No Harm in Talking: Re-Establishing the Relationship between Theological and Secular Bioethics', *The American Journal of Bioethics* 20. 12 (2020) 5-13, here 5.
2. For more detailed information please refer to Maria John P. Selvamani, 'Patient Right to Autonomy Act: A Challenge to Catholic Healthcare in Taiwan', *Lumen: A Journal of Catholic Studies* 9 (2021) (accepted for publication)
3. Chiang Jen-Hsin, 'The Meaning of Life from the Points of Hospice Palliative Care Act and Patient Right to Autonomy Act', *Counseling & Guidance* 404 (2019), 46-52. (in Chinese)
4. Patient Right to Autonomy Act, at https://law.moj.gov.tw/ENG/LawClass/LawAll.aspx?pcode=L0020189 [March 23, 2021]
5. 11 more diseases including cystic fibrosis, Huntington disease and spinal muscular atrophy were added to the list on January 6, 2020 by the Ministry of Health and Welfare. At https://www.mohw.gov.tw/cp-4636-50877-1.html [February 22, 2021]
6. Patient Autonomy Research Center, https://parc.tw/ (in Chinese)
7. https://hpcod.mohw.gov.tw/HospWeb/index.aspx [May 13, 2021]
8. Chen, Shew-Dan, 'An Analysis of Patient Right to Autonomy Act from a Medical Doctor's Perspective', *Applied Ethics Review* 67, (2019): 65-76. (in Chinese); Cheng, Yat-Che and Shih Chao-Jung, 'An Euthanasia - A Brief Comment on the Patient's Self-determination Right Act, Taiwan, 2016'; *The Military Law Journal*, 62 no. 4 (2016): 18-35. (in Chinese)
9. Congregation for the Doctrine of the Faith, 'Responses to Certain Questions Concerning Artificial Nutrition and Hydration' (2007); Pope John Paul II, 'Address to the Participants in the International Congress on Life-Sustaining Treatments and the Vegetative State' (March 20 2004).
10. American Geriatrics Society Ethics Committee and Clinical Practice and Models of Care

Committee, 'American Geriatrics Society Feeding Tubes In Advanced Dementia Position Statement', *Journal of American Geriatrrics Society* 64, no. 8 (2014), https://doi.org/http://dx.doi.org/10.1111/jgs.12924. p.1591

11. Eric Marcelo O. Genilo, 'Church Power and the Reproductive Health Debate in the Philippines', in Yiu Sing Lucas Chan/James F. Keenan/Shaji George Kochuthara (eds), *Doing Asian Theological Ethics in a Cross-Cultural and an Interreligious Context*, Bangalore, Dharmaram Publications, 2016, 277-290.

12. James T. Bretzke, 'Moral Theology Out of East Asia', *Theological Studies*, 61.1 (2000), 106-121 here 113.

13. Elio Gasda, 'Theological Ethics and the People of God: Profile, Tensions and Perspectives', in Antonio Autiero/Laurenti Magesa (eds), *The Catholic Ethicist in the Local Church*, New York, Orbis Books 2018 7-17 here 10

14. Yi-Jhen He, Ming-Hwai Lin, Jo-Lan Hsu, Bo-Ren Cheng, Tzeng-Ji Chen and Shinn-Jang Huang, 'Overview of the Motivation of Advance Care Planning: A Study from a Medical Center in Taiwan', *International Journal of Environmental Research and Public Health*, 18.2 (2021) 417.

15. Shaji George Kochuthara, 'Challenge of Doing Catholic Ethics in a Pluralistic Context', *Religions* 11, no. 1: 17. https://doi.org/10.3390/rel11010017. Here 12.

16. Shih, Zhao-Liang, 'Buddhist Perspective of Patient's Right of Autonomy', *Applied Ethics Review* 68 (2020) 77-100 (in Chinese)

17. Pope Francis, 'Evangelii Gaudium' (November 24, 2013), http://w2.vatican.va/content/francesco/en/apost_exhortations/documents/papa-francesco_esortazione-ap_20131124_evangelii-gaudium.html 213-214. [April 10, 2021] here 49.

Women Decolonising Theologies of, for and by Southeast Asians

SHARON A. BONG

The research aim of this project is to offer a critical interrogation of what constitutes the 'Asianness' of doing Christian theology in Southeast Asia. Based on in-depth interviews conducted with six women theologians in the region, and framed within the broader context of the research project that was aimed at decolonising theology, five 'I's may be inductively gleaned: inadequacy, identity, inter-relationality, inclusiveness, and insistence. The paper shows how these Southeast Asian women theologians re-imagine Christianity as an Asian legacy, as a paradigm shift from situating it as a colonial legacy in Asia. By embracing inter-relationality and inclusiveness, they liberate theology in engendering for us, a feminist-postcolonial theology of just love and radical hospitality.

I teach theology of communication [...] about the Trinity, the source of communication [...] creation and redemption and the whole of salvation [...these are] different ways of God [communicating] with us.[1]

So we danced like Miriam...and I could see their [schoolgirls'] identification [...] with how intelligent Miriam was to save [her people...] so that is doing gender theology.[2]

[My work] is more intentionally decolonising [...] but I don't necessarily polarise.[3]

I intend to develop a deaf ethics [... And] women are more prone to abuse even within the circle of deaf [communities].[4]

Some women [at the Karen Baptist Church], they want to be ordained you know [... but] they think themselves that this menstruation is polluted.[5]

I think take on a much bigger concept of God in terms of a God that expands, that [...] is not limited to a certain gender [...] So now I can actually be more vulnerable and use segments of my own stories [...] I would think authenticity is one [...] So for me, I don't see FCC as a gay church [...] I think of it as an inclusive church.[6]

Who are these Southeast Asian feminist and queer theologians? Why do their theologising, as women, matter? This paper does not seek to address these rhetorical questions but rather seeks to redress the theological gaps that give rise to these questions. Based on these six interview extracts and the broader contexts of the research project that was aimed at decolonising theology, five 'I's may be inductively gleaned: inadequacy, identity, inter-relationality, inclusiveness, and insistence.

Firstly, the knowledge and praxis of many women within theological institutions of learning, theological circles and the faith community as a whole, tend to be unacknowledged, elided or granted token legitimacy. Highly trained women theologians with much field experience in mission are made to feel inadequate. To what extent is this an inadequacy that is deemed ontological; meaning that there is an inherent lack about womanhood and femininity, e.g. a menstruating body is a polluting body? To what extent does the church's theology of the body—regardless of denomination—that is premised on gender complementarity entrench this ontological lack; that women are equal but different? To what extent does the church hold itself accountable for this gender bias that is replicable in society, evidenced through discriminatory cultural practices, e.g. son preference (as the 'girl-child is not appreciated in her family'),[7] child marriage that disproportionately affects girls, and sexual and gender-based violence that disproportionately affects women, as "women are more prone to abuse even within the circle of deaf [communities]"?

Secondly, if as Agnes Brazal, Full Professor in Theology at the De la

Salle University, Philippines posits, that "all theologies are contextual" (elsewhere in the interview), an intersectional identity matters. Identities are heterogeneous as differences that matter include our sex, gender, race, nationality, class, cultural and religious identities. For women theologising in an Asian context, this heterogeneity translates as multiple layers of oppression on account of each of those identity markers; sexism, racism (anti-Asian in the time of Coronavirus), homophobia, transphobia, and xenophobia. But the 'Asian woman' or 'third-world woman' is not a monolithic, fixed and stable identity which Chandra Talpade Mohanty, a feminist-postcolonial theorist, challenges, as there are differences among Asian women.[8] Women theologians balance the universalism of religious truths and the particularities of their social locations and lived realities. In this way, women who engage in contextual theologising have a situated albeit "partial perspective", as Donna Haraway puts it, in avoiding the "god-trick" which refers to the abstraction of knowledge claims.[9] A *"critical relativism"*[10] —which straddles universality and particularity— that emerges, is reflected in Brazal's standpoint; that her work "is more intentionally decolonising [...] but I don't necessarily polarise". She proposes an "ecclesiastical model" of church as a "sacrament of *yin-yang* harmony" that remains consonant with the "theology of harmony" of the Federation of Asian Bishops' Conference, where *yin-yang* is not diametrically opposed to each other but rather mutually constituting.[11]

Whilst recognising Christianity as a colonial heritage (via the Spanish conquest in the context of the Philippines where Brazal continues to theologise from), she, like other women theologians, avoid the pitfall of reinstating polarising binaries like West/East and coloniser/colonised. In fleshing out what it means to be Asian women doing theology in Asia as an everyday practice, it is fitting to foreground Asianness and to simultaneously go beyond that. In reclaiming the right to self-representation, as a counterpoint to being under-represented or misrepresented, it is a challenge to not valorise or exoticise Asianness in our quest for an identity politics that is necessarily premised on differences not only from the West but also within Asia. Chen's 'Asia as method' is instructive in this instance as he calls for a paradigm shift in interrogating the distinctiveness of Asia, not by situating it in dialectical conversation with Europe which is historically overdone, but rather seeing the rest of Asia with a clear eye cast on the diversities and disparities within Asia itself that comprises larger nations and smaller nations, richer economies and poorer ones, those that have been colonized by the 'West' and 'East' (e.g. despotism, military rule).[12] In what ways is Asia bound by commonalities beyond its geographical proximity, even though it does not have a shared language save the English language? Women theologians inflect this means of interrogation with a feminist lens to consider what constitutes the 'Asianness' of Christian feminist theology in Southeast Asia.

Thirdly, inter-relationality for women theologians finds expression in a revisionist understanding of the Trinity as 'the source of communication' which is the springboard from which Maria Ngoc Lan, a member of the Franciscan Missionaries of Mary and Professor of Communication Theology at De La Salle Theological Institute in Sai Gon, develops a "theology of communication". The ordering of the Trinitarian structure is not only masculinised (the amorphous Spirit notwithstanding) but also hierarchized which, in turn, is reflected in the oppositional and hierarchical ordering of male/female. Re-visioning the Trinity as relational disrupts by calling to question the androcentrism of creation. Rev. Naw Htoo Htoo who is currently Professor of Old Testament and Feminist Theology at Karen Baptist Theological Seminary and Chairperson of Karen Baptist Convention Women's Department, adds that 'Jesus is man, but Jesus is a feminist, because you know Jesus stands for women [laughs], fights again for women' (elsewhere in the interview). Re-visioning Christology enables a more intimate identification of Asian women theologians with the figure of Christ who 'stands for women, fights again for women'. This sadly, is dissonant with their everyday realities of encountering gender-based discrimination from their male colleagues, male clerics within and without Churches whose spiritual formation seems to have bypassed feminist theologies as there is seemingly no desire to emulate a feminist Christ. As 'Jesus is a feminist', those who self-identify as feminist in doing theology find meaning and validation where they are positioned and treated as strangers, imposters and trespassers. Julia Ong, an Infant Jesus sister based in Singapore, adds a corrective to the lack of women in leadership roles in churches through creative methodologies used in the classroom with girls, as she says (of one session where she chose to privilege Miriam's rather than Moses' narrative): "So we danced like Miriam [...and] I could see their (schoolgirls') identification [...] with how intelligent Miriam was to save [her people...] so that is doing gender theology". Women recognised and valued as sages, prophetesses, judges and saviours can and have become realities for some across time and space.

Re-visioning the Trinity as relational is further disruptive by calling to question the anthropocentrism of creation. Naw Htoo Htoo speaks of 'ecofeminism' (elsewhere in the interview). Although ecofeminism has been heavily critiqued as essentialist in aligning women with nature; specifically, in drawing a parallelism between the mistreatment of women and the destruction of nature, it serves as a critical counterpoint to environmental policies that are gender-blind: that do not see the inter-relationality between ecological or climate justice and gender justice. Gender-blind environmental policies also elide the contribution of women and indigenous peoples everywhere to the conservation of the earth and its resources, their sustainable everyday practices of toiling the earth as opposed to conglomerates' plundering the earth's finite resources. Faith-based documents such as *Laudato Si'* that still extol man as the centre of the universe fail to recognise the end of the Age of the Anthropocene. The Covid-19 pandemic is, in fact, a symptom of the deep fracturing of relationships between the humans and their ecosystem that is both cause and effect of the desolation and destruction of our 'common home'.

Fourth, inclusiveness is the by-product of embracing inter-relationality as it relates to how we encounter and manage differences. What is common is how differences are mismanaged through the entrenchment of binaries that entail an inferiorisation of secondary terms—male/female, white/non-white, coloniser (Self)/colonised (Native other), able/disabled. haves/haves not, etc. Pauline Ong, who identifies as a 'gay woman' and is currently Executive Pastor of the Free Community Church in Singapore, further dismantles the construct of heteronormative/non-heteronormative, by coming out to herself, her loved ones and the FCC faith community, when she reflects, "on a much bigger concept of God in terms of a God that expands, that [...] is not limited to a certain gender". Such a standpoint goes against the grain of mainstream theology which is not only heteronormative in normalising heterosexuality but also heterosexist in marginalising even demonising other (non-procreative and aberrant) sexualities, e.g. homosexuality, bisexuality, asexuality (which is not synonymous with celibacy), pansexuality, intersexuality, etc. Where she felt inadequate as one whose difference may have been read as defective, she is so affirmed by her Christian faith that it empowers her to "be more vulnerable". In terms of becoming a subject, a person, 'authenticity' is vital in being true to oneself and for many LGBT-identifying persons of faith; this means being able to reconcile one's sexuality with one's spirituality. The deep-seated belief that one is not only created in the image of God but that God is imaged in such a body that many deem as profane is sacralising. And she adds, "I don't see FCC as a gay church [...] I think of it as an inclusive church". Does one encounter inclusiveness only in churches like the FCC?

A 'common home' becomes a problematic notion as it is neither common (due to social divisiveness and injustices) nor homely (due to hostility to 'the stranger') for all, at all times and all spaces. A 'common home' ceases to become a place of refuge or belonging when we cannot see the grace of God flourishing in the bodies of those whom we close-off as 'the stranger'. Rather than embrace the inter-relationality between ourselves and 'the stranger' (e.g. migrant workers, refugees, differently abled bodies, the infirm, the aged and those who are simply not like us), we distance ourselves further from the truth of our shared humanity. How can a 'new humanity'[13] be envisaged when the human family cannot even treat each other with love and compassion: when its house is not in order? It is ironic that a later encyclical (*Fratelli Tutti*) would revert to exhorting the values of inter-relationality among humans where the earlier encyclical (*Laudato Si'*) extolled the values of inter-relationality between human-other human in creation. This seems to suggest how much farther humanity has to go to becoming human and proving its worth as the centre of creation, as custodians of the gift of creation. Pope Francis' vision of our "future [as] not monochrome"[14] in the later encyclical— notwithstanding the seemingly exclusionary call to fraternity (as callout to brethren and men)—authenticates prophetic ways of dealing with our differences, far removed from present ones that lead to division, dispossession and disenfranchisement.

Finally, insistence is a practice that is rooted in resilience and persistence in doing feminist and queer theology in the face of disqualifications, dissension and disunity. All six women theologians as educators and mentors have experienced *metanoia* and seek to recreate that in those whom they encounter. They engage in consciousness-raising of each other (e.g. Agnes Brazal serves as mentor to both Julia Ong and Kristine Meneses), their students, mentees and novices (e.g. Maria Ngoc Lan, was head of the formation team in the Ho Chi Minh City province at the time of the interview). Agnes Brazal, Julia Ong and Kristine Meneses are members of the Ecclesia of Women in Asia which is an academic forum of Asian Catholic feminist women theologians (with Brazal also serving as its co-founder). EWA aims to generate, and make accessible through its post-conference publications,[15] Asian feminist theologies that are grounded in the lived realities of those displaced and dislocated whom they accord epistemic privilege to, e.g. Dalit women, the deaf community, the LGBT community, migrant workers, refugees, sex workers, activists agitating for social justice, etc. They also engage in and engender 'feminist hermeneutics', 'feminist missiology', 'feminist ecclesiology' and 'ecofeminism' not only through EWA's biennial conferences held since 2001 but by '[making] compulsory' these subjects which Naw Htoo Htoo proudly does at the Karen Baptist Theological Seminary where she has taught for the past 22 years. Insistence importantly germinates from self-affirmation that Naw Htoo Htoo professes as she says, "I believe that I am the chosen instrument" (elsewhere in the interview). Insistence also lies in the self-confidence at having found and accepted one's vocation: for Meneses, who is currently affiliated with the Pontifical University of Santo Tomas and former Coordinator of EWA, it is "to develop a deaf ethics" having interpreted mass by using sign language since 2008. She posits that when we truly see the deaf, in "meeting them 'eye-to eye'", as Jesus did (Mark 7:31–37) and experienced a *metanoia,* we are enabled to revision healing by unlearning our internalised "fear of disability" and learning to "love diversity".[16]

Insistence is also playful where we have the lasting impression of Julia Ong dancing with schoolgirls in celebration of their girlhood and tomorrow's women leaders. And insistence is also the realisation that one does not need to be 'authorised', i.e. given (masculine) permission to claim one's 'scope and freedom of speech', especially when one harnesses social media platforms to do so. And her vision, in operationalising as Christian praxis, feminist and liberation theologies or 'funny theologies', is expressed as:

> I really felt this desire, this call and the need to equip the laity and the people with tools for exegesis, doing theology, understanding in order to bring the church up. So I started, I came back (from Mary Hill in the Philippines) and I taught, where I did scripture sessions [...] I was teaching skills. And I was not encouraged.

Similarly, in terms of cultural barriers, Naw Htoo Htoo's persistence in changing mind-sets is a long-term struggle, as she says:

> But male students, they think this subject (feminist theology) is from Western phenomenon and then they have prejudice and bias on this subject. And the problem I noticed is because of the patriarchal system and because of our culture [...] especially we are in a Buddhist environment [...where in Myanmar] men are born with glory. So this becomes the traditional idea [...] that men are always superior to women.

Insistence thus lies in systematically breaking down the binaries of male/female, strong/weak, Western/Eastern, familiar/funny (strange), clerical/laity, Christianity/local cultures, and superior/inferior where women and femininity tend to be aligned with the second and secondary (or derivative) terms. Pauline Ong adds another binary that she has had to personally overcome—heteronormative/non-heteronormative—with a turning point occurring having taken the subject 'Authentic sexuality' at the Singapore Bible College, where the 'six passages'[17] were approached by the 'gracious stance' of a 'conservative' instructor, as she explains:

> And I think that really helped me come to a point of personal reconciliation for myself, between faith and sexuality. I really felt like God was kind of pushing me to do something more. That I had a very unique experience in terms of spirituality, in terms of being a gay woman [...] that I couldn't just keep quiet and not tell my story or not help other younger Christians who may be struggling [...] anyone who deals with a religion [...] because we come from a culture that's very multi-religious and Asia [...] dealing with family, with culture and your

own religion and being gay has always been one of those really difficult areas.

To queer or make unfamiliar is not only a form of insistence but also resistance. It is to call out or challenge structures of oppression when we encounter them and dismantle the systemic violence of sexism, racism, homophobia, transphobia, ableism, and xenophobia, where we can. These women theologians are beacons of light, as they "give voice especially to theologians in the margins or women theologians in the margins" as Brazal puts it. In doing so, they liberate theology in engendering for us an Asian feminist-postcolonial theology of just love and radical hospitality.

In conclusion, an Asian feminist-postcolonial theology of just love and radical hospitality is a decolonising project. It is inductively generated from the narratives and praxis of seven women theologians who are based in Southeast Asia. In drawing from a richer legacy of her stories (Asian feminist-postcolonial theologians who precede them), they call out the androcentric leanings of theological institutions and learning that give rise to feelings of inadequacy and ontological inferiority based on the church's theology of body that is premised on complementarity of the sexes. They show through doing inter-relationality and inclusiveness by re-visioning the Trinitarian structure, and theologising from the lived realities of the least, the last and the lost. In carving a niche for themselves and a safe space for others, similarly deemed unworthy, within the parameters of liberation theologies, they also insist on their feminist standpoint and Asianness that afford them the context from which to theologise from. In these ways, they offer a transformative vision and praxis of just love and radical hospitality that, in decolonising theology, liberates it.

Notes

1. Interview with Maria Ngoc Lan, Franciscan Missionaries of Mary on 15 April 2015 at the Franciscan Missionaries of Mary House, Ho Chi Minh City, Vietnam.
2. Interview Julia Ong, Infant Jesus on 26 April 2015 at the Infant Jesus Convent, Singapore.
3. Interview with Agnes Brazal on 7 May 2015 at St Vincent's School of Theology, Quezon City, Philippines.
4. Interview with Kristine Meneses on 7 May 2015 at St Vincent's School of Theology, Quezon City, Philippines.

5. Interview with Naw Htoo Htoo on 10 June 2015 at the Karen Baptist Theological Seminary, Seminary Hill, Insein, Yangon, Myanmar.
6. Interview with Pauline Ong on 25 April 2015 at the Free Community Church, Singapore.
7. Interview with Julia Ong, IJ.
8. Chandra Talpade Mohanty, 'Under Western Eyes: Feminist Scholarship and Colonial Discourses', *Feminist Review*, 30, 1 (1988), pp. 62–63.
9. Donna Haraway, *Simians, Cyborgs, and Women: The Reinvention of Nature*, New York: Routledge, 1991, pp. 189, 191.
10. Sharon A. Bong, *Becoming Queer and Religious in Malaysia and Singapore*, London and New York: Bloomsbury Academic, 2020, p. 131.
11. Agnes Brazal, 'Church as Sacrament of Yin-Yang Harmony: Toward a More Incisive Participation of Laity and Women in the Church', *Theological Studies*, 80, 2 (2019), 434.
12. Kuan-Hsing Chen, *Asia as Method: Toward Deimperialization*, Durham and London: Duke University Press, 2010, pp. 215, 255.
13. Pope Francis, 'Encyclical Letter *Fratelli Tutti* of The Holy Father Francis on Fraternity and Social Friendship', *Vatican Press*, 3 October 2020, paragraph 127 at: http://www.vatican.va/content/francesco/en/encyclicals/documents/papa-francesco_20201003_enciclica-fratelli-tutti.html
14. Ibid., paragraph 100.
15. One of EWA's eight edited books includes, Agnes M. Brazal and Kochurani Abraham (eds.), *Feminist Cyberethics in Asia: Religious Discourses on Human Connectivity*, New York: Palgrave Macmillan, 2014.
16. Kristine C. Meneses, 'Deafinitely Different: Seeing Deafness, Deaf, and Healing in the Bible from Deaf Perspective', in Robert E. Shore-Goss and Joseph N. Goh (eds.), *Unlocking Orthodoxies for Inclusive Theologies: Queer Alternatives*, London: Routledge, 2020, pp. 187–188.
17. Texts of Terror that are typically used to condemn homosexuality include: Old Testament; Gen 19:5, Lev 18:22 and 20:13 and from the New Testament; Rom 1:24–25, 1 Cor 6:9 and 1 Tim 1:10. See Patrick S. Cheng, 'Rethinking Sin and Grace for LGBT People Today', in Marvin Mahan Ellison and Kelly Brown Douglas (eds.), *Sexuality and the Sacred: Sources for Theological Reflection*, 2nd revised edition. Louisville, Kentucky: Westminster John Knox Press, 2010, 106.

THEOLOGICAL FORUM

Catholicity as a Principle for a Dissenting Church

WILIBALDUS GAUT

Do differences and disagreements in the Church contradict its unity, and should they therefore be avoided? This article, initially presented during the Leuven Encounters in Systematic Theology (LEST) XIII Conference on "Dissenting Church" (October 2021), seeks to address this question by means of the notion of catholicity. I would argue that insofar as the Church's catholicity is carefully concerned, differences and disagreements are not against its unity, but rather lie at the heart of its existence. The notion of catholicity envisions a certain model of the unity of the Church and in turn shapes the way of exercising the Church governance, in which differences and dissents might become commonplace. For this reason, catholicity then underpins the practice of synodality in the Church.

1. Catholicity and the Unity of the Church as Communion

The term catholicity is derived from the Greek adjective *katholikos* that means "universal", and the adverb *kath'holou* which means "on the whole" or "according to the whole".[1] According to Avery Dulles, the universality that the term catholic refers to implies the idea of fullness or integral wholeness.[2] This concept of fullness or integral wholeness, however, does not mean a kind of totality that dismisses every individuality or particularity.

As one of the marks of the Church, according to the Nicene-Constantinopolitan Creed, catholicity might convey a wide range of meanings. Yet, as Dulles points out, it first and foremost speaks of the internal diversity in the Church, which at the same time should be perceived in view of its unity. Herein, catholicity denotes a "reconciled diversity", i.e., a unity that maintains the diversity of its constituting elements and exists by a mutual service and receptivity, as well as a free exchange of trust and respect among them.[3]

Wolfgang Beinert argued that catholicity envisions a certain model of the unity of the Church, which is best explained through the concept of communion. For Beinert, communion as a model of unity in the Church represents what he calls "a multiple figure of unity", whereby "each organ is called to fulfill its irreducible and original function within the whole."[4] In this model of unity, both distinction and mutual relationship are well maintained.

In sum, the dynamic nature of the communion model of unity implies that it is shaped by the complex interactions of its diverse constitutive elements. A prime reference for the concept of communion as a model of the unity of the Church is the image of the Body of Christ in Pauline writings.[5] For instance, Paul writes: "Just as a body, though one, has many parts, but all its many parts form one body, so it is with Christ" (1 Cor. 12:12). Each part, though in distinct ways thanks to their unique functions, equally contributes to the healthy operating of the whole body.

One can therefore go on to argue that with the vision of the active and equal participation of all the constituting elements, the catholic view of unity as communion also promotes the idea of an inclusive and egalitarian community. No one can be excluded or considered less important for every single element assumes equal significance and each distinct contribution is fully recognized. I would argue that such a vision of the Church has a bearing on the way synodal governance should be exercised, as I shall explain in the following section.

2. Synodality as a Catholic Way of Exercising the Church Governance
For the understanding of synodality, I follow the document of the International Theological Commission, *Synodality in the Life and Mission of the Church*.[6] In it, synodality is understood as "the involvement and participation of the whole people of God in the life and mission of the Church." Elsewhere in the document, such an understanding of synodality is clearly recognized as giving expression to the catholicity of the Church as communion. Synodality in the Church, it says, "reveals and gives

substance to her being as communion when all her members journey together, gather in assembly and take an active part in her evangelising mission."[7]

Such a definition of synodality can be attributed to Pope Francis who introduced the concept of "an entirely synodal Church".[8] Synodality, in this sense, calls for the recognition of the place of all the baptized and their role "in the prudential discernment about Church decision-making and governance".[9] The underlying assumption of such a conviction is that all the members of the Church share the fullness of faith, which they attain "by virtue of the dignity of baptism and their friendship with Christ".[10] Advocating the notion of a synodal Church, Pope Francis insists that the concept of the people of God should serve as signifying the key feature of the Church. In so doing, he expresses Vatican II's vision of a participative and dialogical Church.[11]

Putting forth the active participation of its all members, a synodal Church is against any tendency toward an excessive centralization in the Church that allows the entire process of decision-making to be rendered to a few elites.[12] While acknowledging the various roles to play based on different gifts and charisms, synodality stands for the conviction that everyone in the Church is a subject who retains the right to determine the communal life, which is put into practice through their participation in the decision-making on things that pertain to the life of all.[13]

What is particularly notable in this regard is the far-reaching consequences of this synodal way of decision-making. Indeed, to consult people means to allow them to honestly express their different views and perspectives. The synodal process, understood in this way, will turn out to be a complex one, in which dissent and disagreement are commonplace resulting from the differing standpoints and views.

3. A Synodal Church is a Dissenting Church

A synodal Church, as Massimo Faggioli says, "is no longer a Church that pretends to be in absolute agreement on everything," but rather the one "that admits that there are disagreements on important issues".[14] Bradford Hinze shares a similar view. The recognition of the role of conflict and honest speech (*parrhesia*), Hinze argues, is one of the significant achievements of the vision of a synodal Church.[15] So, synodality provides "a way of understanding and experiencing the Church where legitimate differences find room in the logic of a reciprocal exchange of gifts in the light of truth."[16]

One way to understand how differences come to the fore is by taking into consideration that consultation, the medium of active participation of the faithful in the Church, should not be seen separately from the discernment of the Spirit or from reading the signs of the time. This is because the people of God to consult with, are those who are willing to actively listen to what the Holy Spirit is saying and to discern how it resonates with their life circumstances in view of giving an appropriate response to their Christian calling and mission.[17]

This line of argument finds its ground in the awareness that a synodal Church is a missionary Church. A synodal model for governing the Church envisions the realization of God's mission entrusted to the Church through Christ.[18] Faggioli captures this matter well as he writes that "the rediscovery of a more participative ecclesiological model," which is the essence of a synodal Church, aims to reaffirm "a missionary ecclesiology".[19]

The fundamental purpose of the practice of synodality is "to interpret reality with the eyes and heart of God", and only in so doing the Church can properly undertake its mission in today's world.[20] As such, a synodal Church is always cognizant of its call to respond effectively to particular circumstances and all the challenges it poses, and such a response is made "in fidelity to the *depositum fidei* and in creative openness to the voice of the Spirit."[21]

This implies that a synodal Church does take into consideration the concrete experience that surrounds the life and mission of the faithful. Amanda Osheim argued that synodality helps to "foster an understanding of faith incarnated in the diverse cultural and historical contexts characteristic of the Church's catholicity."[22] Pope Francis has expressed a similar view in which he explicitly recognizes the starting point of a synodal Church. He asserts that a synodal Church begins to take shape only when it is persistently "connected to the 'base' and starts from people and their daily problems."[23]

To take people's real experiences as the starting point means to acknowledge the variety of perspectives and the distinctive aspects that shape their lives as a result of differing contexts and circumstances. Osheim regards this practice of synodality an expression of catholicity as a unity that maintains diversity. A synodal process in the Church, she remarks, is "a collaborative process inclusive of divergent voices."[24] Therefore, it should also accommodate dissent and disagreement. As Robert Schreiter put it, catholicity denotes "the ability to hold things together in tension with one another,"[25] and hence it also envisions what Aloys Grillmeier called "a union of opposites".[26]

This model of catholicity strongly promotes pluriformity and upholds decentralization. In this respect, another insight of Hinze is helpful as he links synodality with the notion of polycentrism. A synodal Church, in his view, is of great importance in "promoting a 'healthy decentralization' in the Church and a polycentric approach to the Church's universality."[27] As a result, the decision on certain matters can vary from one context to another. To what extent these decisions can vary, and on which levels of the Church government these variations can be implemented, is a matter of debate on synodality in the period to come.

Notes

1. Richard P. McBrien, *Catholicism* (New York: HarperCollins Publisher, 1994), 3.
2. Avery Dulles, *The Catholicity of the Church* (Oxford: Oxford Unity Press, 1985), 14.
3. Dulles, *The Catholicity of the Church*, 21-25.
4. Woflgang Beinert, 'Catholicity as a Property of the Church', *The Jurist* 52 (1992):470-471.
5. Beinert, 'Catholicity as a Property of the Church', 471.
6. *Synodality in the Life and Mission of the Church* (March 2, 2018), 7, <http://www.vatican.va/roman_curia/congregations/cfaith/cti_documents/rc_cti_20180302_sinodalita_en.html> [Last accessed October 9, 2020].
7. *Synodality in the Life and Mission of the Church*, 6.
8. Pope Francis, 'Address of His Holiness Pope Francis at the Ceremony Commemorating the Fiftieth Anniversary of the Institution of the Synod of Bishops' (October 17, 2015), http://w2.vatican.va/content/francesco/en/speeches/2015/october/documents/papa-francesco_20151017_50-anniversario-sinodo.html [Last accessed October 10, 2017].
9. Daniel P. Horan, 'Synodality as the Only Way to be Church', *National Catholic Reporter*, December 27-January 9 (2020): 16.
10. *Synodality in the Life and Mission*, 25 & 58.
11. Ormond Rush, 'Inverting the Pyramid: The SensusFideliumin a Synodal Church', *Theological Studies* 78/2 (2017): 304-305.
12. Massimo Faggioli, 'From Collegiality to Synodality: Promise and Limits of Francis's 'Listening Primacy", *Irish Theological Quarterly* 85/4 (2020): 354; Cf. Bradford Hinze, 'Can We Find a Way Together?' *Irish Theological Quarterly* 85/3 (2020): 215.
13. *Synodality in the Life and Mission*, 65.
14. Massimo Faggioli, *Catholicism and Citizenship: Political Cultures of the Church in the Twenty-First Century* (Minnesota: Liturgical Press, 2017), 65.

15. Hinze, 'Can We Find a Way Together?', 217, 227-228.
16. *Synodality in the Life and Mission*, 9.
17. *Synodality in the Life and Mission*, 55, 113 & 114; Cf. Amanda C. Osheim, 'Stepping toward a Synodal Church', *Theological Studies* 80/2 (2019): 376.
18. Faggioli, 'From Collegiality to Synodality', 5; Cf. *Synodality in the Life and Mission*, 75-76.
19. Massimo Faggioli, *The Liminal Papacy of Pope Francis: Moving towards Global Catholicity* (New York: Orbis Books, 2020), 134.
20. *Synodality in the Life and Mission*, 120.
21. *Synodality in the Life and Mission*, 94.
22. Osheim, 'Stepping toward a Synodal Church', 373.
23. Francis, 'Address Commemorating'.
24. Osheim, 'Stepping toward a Synodal Church', 379-380.
25. Robert J. Schreiter, *The New Catholicity: Theology between the Global and the Local* (New York: Orbis Books, 1997), 128.
26. Aloys Grillmeier, 'Commentary on Lumen Gentium', in *Commentary on the Documents of Vatican II*, ed. Herbert Vorgrimler (New York: Herder and Herder, 1967), vol. I, 167.

Johann Baptist Metz (1926-2019): A Personal and Critical Tribute

ERIK BORGMAN

December 2, 2019, German theologian Johann Baptist Metz died at the age of 91. During the last period of his life, he has put much energy into editing the texts that he hopes will be his lasting legacy. In 2018, the concluding index volume of his collected writings was published.[1] One hundred and ten pages of it are taken up by his bibliography. Yet he was not a prolific writer. The story goes that Metz told his friend Edward Schillebeeckx (1914-2009) not to write such large books "because there is not that much truth at all". Even if this anecdote were apocryphal, it tells us something about Metz's writings: many relatively short essays that he regularly reprinted more than once with comparatively minor changes in nuance.

Metz was one of the founders of *Concilium*. I present here a brief reflection on the work of this theologian, who always remained a bit of an outsider in contemporary theology but who, partly because of that, is highly important to me.[2]

A reflection on being church

I start with pointing towards a text that is not very well known in the international context, but that was very significant for Metz himself: the fundamental document on the mission of the church that he wrote under the title *Unsere Hoffnung* (6/2:30-56) for the so-called Würz-burg Synod (1971-1975). The purpose of that Synod was to draw conclusions from the Second Vatican Council for the dioceses of the German Federal Republic. The text was accepted by the Synod with the usual changes and published anonymously but the fact that Metz was the original author was generally known. He himself returned to the document frequently in later articles. Apparently, it was important to him to know that he not simply vented some ideas of his own, but that he represented a vision that was recognizable as authentic in the church.

Now, more than 45 years later, this 'Confession of Faith for our Time' (6/2:30-56) is still impressive because of the honesty with which the position of faith and church are confronted. A renewed focus on following Jesus Christ is presented as an answer to the burning questions of the moment. The document proclaims that hope for the world is to be found in Jesus but that both the desire for it and its resonance permeate the general culture. The church must neither adapt to the culture nor entrench itself in a one-sided negative cultural critique. It must, like Jesus, insert itself into society without restraint and without fear of being misunderstood. This will inevitably happen, as it happened to him. Safety is not given to the church, as it was not given to the One in whose footsteps it is called to walk, the document stated.

Talking about God
In 1995, on the occasion of the twentieth anniversary of *Unsere Hoffnung*, Metz gave an interview to the German Catholic News Agency KNA. "We should finally start talking about God" is the headline. Metz says he perceives among clergy and people within the church what he calls a *Nachfolgeverweigerung* (nonconformity) and says that demands by progressive Catholics to reform the church are "too much liberalizing". He advocates a risky God-talk, for the crisis of God, he says, is the origin of the crisis in both church and society (8:167-169). Statements like this by Metz in the 1990s were not very well received or understood. But as Metz reveals five years later, again in an interview with KNA, this period is no longer about ways out of the crisis but about ways into the crisis (8:189-191). In 2005, in an interview with the *Süddeutsche Zeitung*, he gave a remarkably mild evaluation of the pontificate of John Paul II and predicted that the then newly elected Benedict XVI might well cause surprises (8:218-223). The latter, as Cardinal Ratzinger, had blocked Metz being appointed in Munich in 1980 and was at least partly responsible for the climate in which several of his students had clashed harshly

with the Magisterium. Nevertheless, Ratzinger was invited to speak at a symposium organized by Metz' students on the occasion of his seventieth birthday, and he did in fact come.

Conversion to suffering

The joint appearance of the two supposed opposites was remarkable, also in view of the history of *Concilium*, Metz's involvement in it and Ratzinger's choice for the competing *Communio,* and it was seen as surprising and even shocking at the time. It was framed as an un-masking convergence of "left" and "right" cultural criticism. In the face of democracy, they continued to cling to an unassailable authority, with the only difference that for Ratzinger this resided in the church and its Magisterium, for Metz it was located in suffering and those who suffer. Hans Küng (1928-2021) saw the encounter as a betrayal of the necessary church renewal, while Metz, for his part, left no doubt that he saw no benefit in Küng's *Projekt Weltethos*.[3] He contrasted this with his own "compassion as a world program of Christianity" (see 4:156-163). Metz's contribution to the conversation with Ratzinger at the time (5:35-50), however, by no means marked a break in his development. For him, history was never a gradual progression towards freedom, with the full implementation of human rights as its fulfilment. He spoke in remarkably positive terms about the empirical church and its "elephant memory", but Metz was always more ecclesial and, if you will, more "pious" than he was often given credit for. In an interview, he made clear how much sustained prayer was the basis of his theologizing (8:75-92) and his whole theology can be reconstructed from there.[4] In my estimation, Metz's attitude towards Ratzinger showed spiritual greatness, and insight. Times had indeed changed and it should be clear that not every fundamental criticism of modernity can be dismissed as reactionary.

In the *Festschrift* for Metz's ninetieth birthday, the pianist Claudius Tanski narrates how Metz's meeting with Ratzinger, and their passionate debate about God, led him to take the long-delayed step of becoming a Catholic. He calls Metz a warrior struggling with God: "this struggle includes reasoning, doubt, denunciation and question, but in a deep ground of faith and trust in the Lord's blessing."[5] It is, I think, an apt characterization of Metz's commitment to theology. He first of all develops a faithful vision from which theology can spring in a renewed way, in confrontation with the world and the prevailing visions of it. His texts are usually not directly helpful in figuring out what needs to be said theologically, and certainly not how it can be argued convincedly. Metz however does not shy away from stressing the need for theologians for what his student and friend Tiemo Rainer Peters (1938-2017) has called a *conversio at passionem*.[6] He impresses upon us that we must theologize face to face with suffering, and adjust not only the content but also the nature of our speaking accordingly. As a result, his texts can seem somewhat monotonous and redundant when read in rapid succession. It remains important, however, to take them up regularly in order to keep theology on track.

Memory of suffering as a way of opening the future
Metz did not write many books. His most famous and indeed most fundamental work is *Glaube in Geschichte und Gesellschaft: Studien zu einer praktischen Fundamentaltheologie,* dating from 1977 (3/1). In it he engages in a profound confrontation with the Critical Theory of the Frankfurt School. This made it clear to him that the Enlightenment and modernity not only marked a growth in empowerment and freedom but also created new forms of disempowerment and serfdom. On the basis of this dialectical view of the Enlightenment process, Metz elaborates his concept of a political theology, as well as that of the church with what he calls an "institution of socio-critical freedom". In an article first published in 1972 in the Dutch-Flemish *Tijdschrift voor Theologie,* Metz distinguishes three models for what he then still calls a "theology of the world" (3/2:90-101). Firstly, there is a theological legitimation of the independence of secular thought that reduces the field on which Christianity has something to say to the inner person. There is, secondly, a commitment to use modern thought as a norm even within theology. And there is what Metz here calls "an eschatological-political theology" that:

> seeks to interpret the surviving forms of Christianity as critically liberating, 'dangerous' memories of freedom and thus to mobilize them within what has been set in motion in the new age of emancipation, secularization and Enlightenment (3/2: 92).

The latter indicates what he himself understands by political theology:

"the attempt to express the eschatological message of Christianity within the relations of the new age as a form of critical-practical thinking".

In *Glaube in Geschichte und Gesellschaft* (3/1), this leads to the statement that the credibility of theology depends on its connection with the practical witness of hope. In that connection it shows itself as "a theology of the world" but at the same time as "exterritorialy opposed to the system" (3/1:34). This leads Metz to proclaim the primacy of praxis (3/1:72-83), to his appreciation of memory and narrative over abstract and subjectless thought as a way to truth (3/1:83-94), and to a theological focus on life and the becoming of all people as free subjects (3/1:97-101). For Metz, the ongoing history of excessive suffering renders implausible not only any linear belief in progress but also any purely argumentative soteriology (3/1:138-149). As an alternative to this, he elaborates the concept of dangerous memory (3/1:105-115) and argues that theologically speaking, the hope for the future is born from the memory of suffering (3/1:116-133). From there, he argues for a renewed engagement with apocalypticism because, as he says, "Jesus' call 'Follow me' and the call of Christians 'Come, Lord Jesus' cannot be separated" (3/1:182-192, cit. 189). For Metz the content of the *memoria passionis* is "the anticipation of a certain future of humanity as a future of those who suffer, the hopeless, the oppressed, the damaged, and the useless of this world" (3/1:133).

Not soteriology but theodicy?
With gratitude I realize how much these and similar thoughts have decisively influenced not only my theology, but my faith as well. However, to end with a critical note, I was less impressed with Metz's book *Memoria passionis*, dating from 2006 and compiled with the help of Johann Reikerstorfer (Volume 4). It is an attempt to present what Metz believes Christianity has to say in the then current cultural situation. Metz argues out-and-out for the memory of suffering to be central, calls for what a theodicy-sensitive theology that stems from missing God[7] – which is important, not to say, necessary. This plea remains rather abstract in this book, however, and it contains few traces of concrete histories and experiences of suffering. On the one hand, Metz tries to hold on to the

idea that in God the hope of comprehensive justice is actualized, an idea that comes from the philosophy of Immanuel Kant (1724-1804) rather than from the memory and narrative traditions of Judaism and Christianity. The fact that this comprehensive justice is actually still far away leads to God being missed. Whereas in *Glaube in Geschichte und Gesellschaft* the memory of suffering becomes visible as a form of hope, suffering in *Memoria passionis* is primarily presented as an incitement to compassion, co-suffering. Against what Metz saw at the time as postmodern amnesia and the "welcoming of religion-friendly godlessness" (5:205-215) that comforts but does not challenge or oblige, he underscores that Christianity does not first and foremost make us happy, but responsible. In what he says about the meaning of Jesus, any suggestion that it would mediate redemption or liberation is treated with suspicion. "It is [...] not primarily soteriology that is at stake, but theodicy," Metz even says (4:64). "Not salvation, but awareness of what is unredeemed."[8] Metz does this with the victims of Auschwitz in mind and emphasizes that reflection on this should be less about forgiving the guilt of the perpetrators than about saving the victims. This is a meaningful position within the German debate as far as I am concerned,[9] but the opposition between redemption and forgiveness seems to me ultimately alien to the New Testament. There, forgiveness for offenders is part of and possible thanks to the connection with the ongoing salvation of the victims.

Going with Metz beyond Metz

For Metz, *Memoria passionis* is in fact always about empathizing with the suffering of others (*das Eingedenken fremden Leids*). Only the desperate cry of absolute lack, he says, gives access to what Christianity is all about (4:95-108). In the course of the history of the Church, *Heilsegoïsmus* (salvation egotism) has proven to be a real danger, but the realization that one's own life cannot be lived truthfully either in the given circumstances can be a profound reason for solidarity. The call to place the suffering of others at the center runs the risk of becoming moralistic, and the constantly repeated claim that our culture forgets the apocalyptic nature of suffering, risks sounding like too massive and ultimately hollow an accusation.

Metz has little inclination for detailed analyses of Scripture or contemporary experiences of suffering. As a result, the interruption of

Johann Baptist Metz (1926-2019): A Personal and Critical Tribute

history he advocates easily remains schematic and does not clearly reveal how it provides an impetus to encounter the God who makes all things new (cf. Rev. 21:5). It is unfortunate that Metz has never engaged deeply with concrete stories of suffering, or with the way in which, according to Latin American liberation theology in particular, the preferential option for the poor is an access to universal salvation, precisely also for non-poor people. But he points at the necessity to do so almost everywhere in his oeuvre.

Notes

1. Metz' collected works are published with Herder in Freiburg as Johann Baptist Metz Gesammelte Schriften (JBMGS). These are its volumes: 1. *Mit dem Gesicht zur Welt* (2015); 2. *Frühe Schriften, Entwürfe und Begriffe* (2015); 3/1. *Im dialektischen Prozess der Aufklärung – Glaube in Geschichte und Gesellschaft: Studien zu einer praktischen Fundamentaltheologie* (2016); 3/2. *Im dialektischen Prozess der Aufklärung: Neue Politische Theologie – Versuch eines Korrektivs der Theologie* (2016); 4. *Memoria passionis: Ein provozierendes Gedächtnis in pluralistischer Gesellschaft* (2017); 5. *Gott in Zeit* (2017); 6/1. *Lerngemeinschaft Kirche: Kirchliche Lernprozesse* (2016); 6/2. *Lerngemeinschaft Kirche: Lernorte – Lernzeiten* (2016); 7. *Mystik der offenen Augen* (2017); 8. *Gespräche, Interview, Antworten: Eine Auswahl* (2017); 9. *Nach-Worte, Bibliografie und Gesamtregister* (2018). References are made in parentheses by indicating the number of the volume and, after a colon, the number of the pages.
2. Being first and foremost a student of Edward Schillebeeckx, I identify with the idea that his position and that of Metz are complementary, as stated in S.M. Roderborn, *Hope in Action: Subversive Eschatology in the Theology of Edward Schillebeeckx and Johann Baptist Metz*, Minneapolis: Fortress 2014.
3. Cf. H. Küng, *Projekt Weltethos*, München: Piper 1990.
4. Cf. A. Prevot, *Thinking Prayer: Theology and Spirituality Amid the Crisis of Modernity*, Notre Dame: University of Notre Dame Press 2015, 165-217 reconstructs Metz' theology based on his anthropology. According to Prevot, the influence of Heidegger plays an important role.
5. C. Tanski, 'Johann Baptist zum 90er!', in *Theologie in gefährdeter Zeit: Stichworte von nahen und fernen Weggefährten für Johann Baptist Metz zum 90. Geburtstag*, Münster: LIT 20192, 514-516, cit. 515.
6. T.R. Peters, 'Conversio ad passionem', in *Wahrheit: Recherchen zwischen Hochscholastik und Postmoderne*, Hg. U. Engel, T. Eggensperger, Mainz: Matthias-Grünewald-Verlag 1995, 274-275.
7. Cf. T.R. Peters, Johann Baptist Metz, *Theologie des vermißten Gottes*, Mainz 1998, 83-92.
8. For details on Metz's Chrstology and soteriology, see J. H. Tück, *Christologie und Theodizee bei Johann Baptist Metz: Ambivalenz der Neuzeit im Licht der Gottesfrage*, Paderborn: Schöning 1999; P. Budi Kleden, Christologie in *Fragmenten: die Rede von Jesus Christus im Spannungsfeld von Hoffnungs- und Leidensgeschichte bei Johann Baptist Metz*, Münster: LIT 2001.
9. Cf. B, Krondorfer, K. von Kellenbach, N. Reck, *Mit Blick auf die Täter: Fragen an die deutsche Theologie nach 1945*, Gütersloh: Gütersloher Verlagshaus 2003.

Contributors

PETER C. PHAN has earned three doctorates and currently is the inaugural holder of the Ignacio Ellacuría Chair of Catholic Social Thought at Georgetown University, Washington, DC, USA.
  Address: 5160 California Lane, Alexandria, VA 22304, USA
  Email: pcp5@georgetown.edu

HUANG PO HO is currently Director of Academy for Contextual Theologies in Taiwan, and editorial board member of *Concilium*. He is also serving as adjunct professor of Claremont School of Theology USA, and Chang Jung Christian University at Taiwan.
  Address: No. 6-5, Ln. 685, Xiaodong Rd., Yongkang Dist., Tainan City 710 , Taiwan
  Email: cjcupekho@gmail.com

CATHERINE CORNILLE is Professor of Comparative Theology at Boston College, where she holds the Newton College Alumnae Chair of Western Culture. Her areas of research focus on Theology of Religions, Comparative Theology, Interreligious Dialogue, and Religious Hybridity. She is the author of *The Im-Possibility of Interreligious Dialogue* (2008) and *Meaning and Method in Comparative Theology* (2020). Her edited volumes include *Many Mansions? Multiple Religious Belonging and Christian Identity* (2002), *Interreligious Hermeneutics* (2010), *Women and Interreligious Dialogue* (2013), *The Wiley-Blackwell Companion to Interreligious Dialogue* (2013) and *Atonement and Comparative Theology* (2021). She is founding and managing editor of the book series "Christian Commentaries on non-Christian Sacred Texts."
  Address; 140 Commonwealth Ave, Chestnut Hill, MA 02467, USA
  Email: cornille@bc.edu

Contributors

THIERRY-MARIE COURAU OP is a Dominican brother, priest, engineer, honorary dean of the faculty of theology and religious studies – the Theologicum – of the Institut Catholique de Paris. His research and publications deal with Buddhism, the theology of dialogue and soteriology. A recent book is *Le salut commedia-logue. De saint Paul VI à François*, Paris, 2018.
   Address: Couvent de l'Annonciation, 222 rue du Faubourg Saint-Honoré, F – 75008 Paris, France
   Email: tm.courau@icp.fr

KATIA LENEHAN is the author of *Beauty and Goodness in Jacques Maritain's Theory of Art* and *The Education of Man: On the Liberal Education of Jacques Maritain*, articles in English (such as 'Theory of Non-Emotion in the Zhuangzi and Its Connection to Wei-Jin Poetry', 'The Role of Aesthetics in Moral Education: A Discussion of Maritain's Philosophy of Education and Art', 'The Human Being as a Unity in Aesthetic Perception and its Possible Meaning for Aesthetic Education in the Global Age', 'The Human Being with Dignity in a Global Age: An Aesthetic Approach') and other articles in Chinese.
   Address: 8F, 178, Ying Zhuang Rd., Danshui Dist., New Taipei City, Taiwan
   Email address: katiaho@hotmail.com

YA-TANG CHUANG, a native Taiwanese, studied philosophy and graduated from Tunghai University, Taichung, Taiwan, with degrees of B.A., M.A., and Ph.D in Philosophy. He studied theology and graduated from Tainan Theological College and Seminary with M. Div. degree and from Princeton Theological Seminary with a degree of M.Th. Currently He is a professor of theology in Department of Theology, the dean of College of Humanities and Social Sciences and dean of the School of Theology, Chang Jung Christian University, Tainan, Taiwan.
   Address: Prof. Ya-Tang Chuang, Chang Jung Christian University, No.1, Changda Rd., Gueiren Dist., Tainan City 71101, Taiwan
   Email: ytchuang487879@gmail.com

DANIEL FRANKLIN PILARIO is member of the Congregation of the Mission and professor of St. Vincent School of Theology (Adamson University) in Manila, Philippines. On weekends, he also works at the garbage dump parish in Payatas, Quezon City. He is the holder of the Vincentian Chair for Social Justice 2021-2022 in St. John's University, New York. A founding member and former President of the Catholic Theological Society of the Philippines (DAKATEO), he is also a member of the Board of Editors of *Concilium* since 2011.

Address: Daniel Franklin Pilario, CM, St. Vincent School of Theology, 221 Tandang Sora Avenue, 1116 Quezon City, Philippines

Email: danielfranklinpilario@yahoo.com

TRAN VAN DOAN studied Philosophy, Sciences and Theology in Rome, Paris, Innsbruck and Tuebingen, and has a PhD in Philosophy (Innsbruck, 1975). Tran has taught philosophy in many universities in Asia and Europe such as the University of Vienna, Peking University, Salzburg University, Vietnam National University, and others as Visiting Professor. He was an Ordinarius of Philosophy at National Taiwan University (1985-2014), a Dean of Theology Faculty at Chang Jung Christian University (2016-2019). Currently, Tran is holding the position of Research Professor at the Academia Catholica (Fujen Catholic University) and Regular Professor at the Catholic College of Vietnam. He has published over 15 books, among them *Reason, Rationality, Reasonableness* (Washington DC: RVP, 2000) and *The Poverty of Ideological Education* (Washington DC: RVP, 2000).

Email: tran@ntu.edu.tw

ANTONY JOHN BAPTIST, Catholic Priest from Vellore, India, holds a Licentiate from the Pontifical Biblical Institute, Rome and a doctorate from state University of Madras. Currently he is the Director of National Biblical Catechetical and Liturgical Centre (NBCLC), Bengaluru. He is also on the Editorial Board of Concilium. Author of many books and numerous articles, John Baptist also served at Sacred Heart Seminary Poonamallee, Chennai, Tamil Nadu Bishop's Council and Conference of the Catholic Bishops of India (CCBI).

Address: Rev. Dr. A. John Baptist, NBCLC, Post Bag 8426, Hutchins Road, 2nd Cross, Bangalore – 560 084, Karnataka, India

Email id:ajbaptist@gmail.com

Contributors

MARIA JOHN P. SELVAMANI is Associate Professor and Dean of Fu Jen Catholic University, Taiwan. He holds a doctorate in molecular biology and bachelor degrees in philosophy and theology. He has authored a book titled *Catholic Faith and Evolution* (2016), and has published journal articles on science and religion and Catholic theological ethics. His research interests are science and religion, and biomedical ethics.
   Address: Fu Jen Catholic University, 150 Zhong Zheng Rd., Hsinzhuang Dist, New Taipei City, Taiwan.
   Email: 058238@mail.fju.edu.tw

SHARON A. BONG is Associate Professor of Gender Studies at the School of Arts and Social Sciences, Monash University, Malaysia. She graduated with a Ph.D. in Religious Studies (2002) and M.A. in Women and Religion (1997), University of Lancaster, UK. She has authored *Becoming Queer and Religious in Malaysia and Singapore* (2020), *The Tension Between Women's Rights and Religions: The Case of Malaysia* (2006) and co-edited *Gender and Sexuality Justice in Asia* (2020) and edited *Trauma, Memory and Transformation in Southeast Asia* (2014). She is former coordinator of the Ecclesia of Women in Asia, a forum writer for the Catholic Theological Ethics in the World Church and member of the *Concilium* Board of Editors.
   Address: School of Arts & Social Sciences, Monash University Malaysia, Jalan Lagoon Selatan, 47500 Bandar Sunway, Selangor Darul Ehsan, Malaysia
   Email: Sharon.bong@monash.edu

WILIBALDUS GAUT is an Indonesian national and currently a PhD researcher at the Department of Systematic Theology, Faculty of Theology and Religious Studies of KU Leuven, Belgium. He is a member of the Research Group of Fundamental Theology and Political Theology. His current PhD research focuses on the notion of catholicity to develop a theological response to globalization with a specific reference to the tension between universalism and particularism as the dual legacy of globalization.
   Address: Tiensestraat 112, Bus 001, 3000 Leuven, Belgium
   Email: wilibaldus.gaut@kuleuven.be

Contributors

ERIK BORGMAN (born 1957, Amsterdam) is a Dutch Lay Dominican and professor of Public Theology at Tilburg University, the Netherlands. At the Radboud University Nijmegen, the Netherlands, he was the Director of the Heyendaal Institute, an institute for interdisciplinary research. He is a former member of the board of editors of *Concilium* and was editor in chief of the Dutch-Flemish journal *Tijdschrift voor Theologie*. He is the biographer of the Flemish theologian Edward Schillebeeckx (1914-2009). He has written numerous articles and books on current theological and societal issues. His most recent books are *Leven van wat komt: Een katholiek uitzicht op de samenleving* (*Living from What Is Coming to Us: A Catholic View on Society*, 2017) and *Alle dingen nieuw: Een theologische visie voor de 21ste eeuw (All Things New: A Theological Vision for the 21st Century)*, 2020.
   Address: Dante office D 104 l, PO Box 90153 l NL - 5000 LE Tilburg
   Email: e.p.n.m.borgman@tilburguniversity.edu

Vision & Mission

What *Concilium* is
Concilium is a journal of Catholic and Ecumenical theological reflection. Founded in the wake of the Second Vatican Council, it seeks to reinterpret and re-apply its vision of openness to new cultural contexts, and to changing social and religious realities. Led by the Spirit, the journal embraces multiple expressions of faith and spirituality arising from cultural plurality as a mark of its catholicity.

The aim of the journal
The aim of *Concilium* is to contribute to the transformation of the world and the Church in light of the Gospel. The journal is particularly committed to challenging structures of oppression and discrimination, and to doing theology from the perspective of the victims of social, economic and ecological inequality. It thus supports a new ecclesial imagination beyond patriarchy, clericalism, racism, anthropocentrism, monocultural hegemony, and the exploitation of the earth's resources.

The way we do theology
The mission of *Concilium* is reflected in the conciliar way of doing theology that we adopt as a community of theologians from various contexts. Inspired by the vision of the journal's founders, we provide a meeting place for a global conversation inviting diverse perspectives on important theological issues. Theologizing from the perspective of the margins and of ecological care are central commitments of *Concilium*. Thus, the journal *Concilium* and its conferences seek to draw attention to the voices and the theological questions and concerns of local and regional communities in a spirit of listening. Our meetings and structures aim to represent collegiality, shared leadership, mutuality, and transparency of decision making. As editors, we are committed to fair and sustainable

relationships among ourselves and with our publishers, readers and authors.

Academic standards and digital presence
Concilium's journal issues strive to maintain academic standards. We remain connected to and draw deeply from the experiences and wisdom of marginalized communities. In order to further our mission, we seek to expand beyond traditional print media and develop a robust digital presence to improve access and participation.

Concilium Subscription Information

April   2022/2: *Covid-19: Beyond the Anthropocene?*

July   2022/3: *Contextual Biblical Interpretation*

October   2022/4: *Theology of Animals*

December   2022/5: *Hospitality and Friendship Today*

February   2023/1: *African Theological Perspectives*

New subscribers: to receive the next five issues of Concilium please copy this form, complete it in block capitals and send it with your payment to the address below. Alternatively subscribe online at www.conciliumjournal.co.uk

Please enter my annual subscription for Concilium starting with issue 2022/2.

Individuals
____ £52 UK
____ £75 overseas and (Euro €92, US $110)

Institutions
____ £75 UK
____ £95 overseas and (Euro €120, US $145)

Postage included – airmail for overseas subscribers

Payment Details:
Payment can be made by cheque or credit card.
a. I enclose a cheque for £/$/€ ____ Payable to Hymns Ancient and Modern Ltd
b. To pay by Visa/Mastercard please contact us on +44(0)1603 785911 or go to www.conciliumjournal.co.uk

Contact Details:
Name ....
Address ....
....
Telephone .... E-mail ....

Send your order to *Concilium*, Hymns Ancient and Modern Ltd
13a Hellesdon Park Road, Norwich NR6 5DR, UK
E-mail: concilium@hymnsam.co.uk
or order online at www.conciliumjournal.co.uk

Customer service information
All orders must be prepaid. Your subscription will begin with the next issue of Concilium. If you have any queries or require Information about other payment methods, please contact our Customer Services department.

CONCILIUM
International Journal of Theology

FOUNDERS
Antoine van den Boogaard; Paul Brand; Yves Congar, OP; Hans Küng;
Johann Baptist Metz; Karl Rahner, SJ; Edward Schillebeeckx

BOARD OF DIRECTORS
President: Thierry-Marie Courau OP
Vice-Presidents: Susan Abraham, Carlos Mendoza-Álvarez OP, Stefanie Knauss,
Daniel Franklin Pilario CM

BOARD OF EDITORS
Susan Abraham, Los Angeles (USA)
Michel Andraos, Chicago (USA)
Antony John Baptist, Bangalore (India)
Michelle Becka, Würzburg (Germany)
Sharon A. Bong, Selangor (Malaysia)
Bernadeth Caero Bustillos, Osnabrück (Germany)
Catherine Cornille, Boston (USA)
Thierry-Marie Courau OP, Paris (France)
Geraldo Luiz De Mori SJ, Belo Horizonte (Brazil)
Margareta Gruber OSF, Vallendar (Germany)
Stan Chu Ilo, Chicago (USA)
Gustáv Kovacs, Pecs (Hungary)
Huang Po-Ho, Tainan (Taiwan)
Stefanie Knauss, Villanova (USA)
Carlos Mendoza-Álvarez OP, Ciudad de México (Mexico)
Esther Mombo, Limuru (Kenya)
Gianluca Montaldi FN, Brescia (Italy)
Daniel Franklin Pilario CM, Quezon City (Philippines)
Carlos Schickendantz, Santiago (Chile)
Stephan van Erp OP, Leuven (Belgium)

PUBLISHERS
SCM Press (London, UK)
Matthias-Grünewald Verlag (Ostfildern, Germany)
Editrice Queriniana (Brescia, Italy)
Editorial Verbo Divino (Estella, Spain)
EditoraVozes (Petropolis, Brazil)

Concilium Secretariat:
Couvent de l'Annonciation
222 rue du Faubourg Saint-Honoré
75008 – Paris (France)
secretariat.concilium@gmail.com
Executive secretary: Gianluca Montaldi FN

http://www.concilium.in

The Canterbury Dictionary of **HYMNOLOGY** The result of over ten years of research by an international team of editors, The Canterbury Dictionary of Hymnology is the major online reference work on hymns, hymn-writers and traditions.

www.hymnology.co.uk

CHURCH TIMES The Church Times, founded in 1863, has become the world's leading Anglican newspaper. It offers professional reporting of UK and international church news, in-depth features on faith, arts and culture, wide-ranging comment and all the latest clergy jobs. Available in print and online.

www.churchtimes.co.uk

Crucible Crucible is the Christian journal of social ethics. It is produced quarterly, pulling together some of the best practitioners, thinkers, and theologians in the field. Each issue reflects theologically on a key theme of political, social, cultural, or environmental significance.

www.cruciblejournal.co.uk

JLS Joint Liturgical Studies offers a valuable contribution to the study of liturgy. Each issue considers a particular aspect of liturgical development, such as the origins of the Roman rite, Anglican Orders, welcoming the Baptised, and Anglican Missals.

www.jointliturgicalstudies.co.uk

magnet Magnet is a resource magazine published three times a year. Packed with ideas for worship, inspiring artwork and stories of faith and justice from around the world.

www.ourmagnet.co.uk

For more information on these publications visit the websites listed above or contact **Hymns Ancient & Modern:**
Tel.: +44 (0)1603 785 910
**Write to: Subscriptions, Hymns Ancient & Modern,
13a Hellesdon Park Road, Norwich NR6 5DR**

www.ingramcontent.com/pod-product-compliance
Lightning Source LLC
Chambersburg PA
CBHW011148290426
44109CB00024B/2536